ADVANCE PRAISE FOR

Home Sweet Zero Energy Home

I attempted my first net zero energy home in 1995 and
quickly learned that designing and building a net zero energy
home requires extensive knowledge of energy efficiency, residential
renewable energy, and green building. This book provides an excellent
overview of these and other vital topics that will help readers
make choices to reach their goals of building the greenest,
healthiest, and most sustainable homes on the planet.

— DAN CHIRAS, director of The Evergreen Institute
and author of *The Homeowner's Guide to Renewable Energy,
Power from the Sun, Power from the Wind*, and many more books
on residential renewable energy and green building

Net zero and zero carbon buildings are the wave of the future.
If you want a house that costs you next to nothing (or nothing) to
heat, cool and operate, Rehfeld's book is an excellent guide for home
owners. From passive solar design, walls, windows, appliances and
government grants, *Home Sweet Zero Energy Home* provides a
comprehensive outline of how to build your own zero energy house.

— GODO STOYKE, author of *The Carbon Charter* and
The Carbon Buster's Home Energy Handbook

Home Sweet Zero Energy Home illustrates the bright future of
mainstream home building as it evolves to incorporate the goal of zero
net energy use without exceeding the cost barriers which have hindered it
in the past. Mr. Rehfeld cuts through the technical jargon and examines
the key topics and information necessary to transform this once esoteric
building strategy into a new paradigm for our standard way of building.

— DAVID A. PILL AIA
Pill - Maharam Architects
Architect/Owner of a Zero Net Energy Home

HOME SWEET ZERO ENERGY HOME

What it takes to **develop great homes** that won't cost anything to **heat, cool** or **light up**, without going **broke** or **crazy**

BARRY REHFELD

NEW SOCIETY PUBLISHERS

Cover design by Diane McIntosh.
Blueprint background © iStock (Nicholas Belton).

Printed in Canada. First printing November 2011.

Paperback ISBN: 978-0-86571-698-8
eISBN: 978-1-55092-492-3

Inquiries regarding requests to reprint all or part of *Home Sweet Zero Energy Home* should be addressed to New Society Publishers at the address below.

To order directly from the publishers, please call toll-free (North America) 1-800-567-6772, or order online at www.newsociety.com

Any other inquiries can be directed by mail to:

New Society Publishers
P.O. Box 189, Gabriola Island, BC V0R 1X0, Canada
(250) 247-9737

Library and Archives Canada Cataloguing in Publication

Rehfeld, Barry J.

Home sweet zero energy home : what it takes to develop great homes that won't cost anything to heat, cool or light up, without going broke or crazy / Barry Rehfeld.

Includes index.
ISBN 978-0-86571-698-8

1. Dwellings--Energy consumption. 2. Dwellings--Energy conservation.
3. Renewable energy sources. 4. Sustainable living. I. Title.

TJ163.5.D86R44 2011   644   C2011-906373-5

New Society Publishers' mission is to publish books that contribute in fundamental ways to building an ecologically sustainable and just society, and to do so with the least possible impact on the environment, in a manner that models this vision. We are committed to doing this not just through education, but through action. The interior pages of our bound books are printed on Forest Stewardship Council-registered acid-free paper that is **100% post-consumer recycled** (100% old growth forest-free), processed chlorine free, and printed with vegetable-based, low-VOC inks, with covers produced using FSC-registered stock. New Society also works to reduce its carbon footprint, and purchases carbon offsets based on an annual audit to ensure a carbon neutral footprint. For further information, or to browse our full list of books and purchase securely, visit our website at: www.newsociety.com

NEW SOCIETY PUBLISHERS

For Elizabeth

Books for Wiser Living
recommended by *Mother Earth News*

TODAY, MORE THAN EVER BEFORE, our society is seeking ways to live more conscientiously. To help bring you the very best inspiration and information about greener, more sustainable lifestyles, *Mother Earth News* is recommending select New Society Publishers books to its readers. For more than 30 years, *Mother Earth* has been North America's "Original Guide to Living Wisely," creating books and magazines for people with a passion for self-reliance and a desire to live in harmony with nature. Across the countryside and in our cities, New Society Publishers and *Mother Earth* are leading the way to a wiser, more sustainable world. For more information, please visit MotherEarthNews.com

Contents

Join the Conversation

Visit our online book club at NewSociety.com to share your thoughts about *Home Sweet Zero Energy Home*. Exchange ideas with other readers, post questions for the author, respond to one of the sample questions or start your own discussion topics. See you there!

1

Free and Clear

IF YOU WERE driving through the small town of Townsend, Massachusetts, along Highland Street in the spring of 2011, you would have passed the future of building just off the side of the road. You *would* have passed it, too, because at thirty miles an hour the small new development looks the same as any other small middle-class neighborhood you'd see in New England.

The nearly two dozen houses already built and occupied are a typical collection of robin egg blue, canary yellow, warbler gray and cardinal red single- and two-story clapboard homes with steep gabled roofs. Had you taken a right, though, on to Coppersmith Way, the development's single road, you'd have seen almost immediately one of the rarest of sights in any single community.

All but one of the homes have solar panels — visibly darker and shinier than the gabled roofs they cover on one side. Towards the end of the lane, you would have seen a nearly completed house that on close inspection had some other uncommon features: unusually deep walls and windows that are noticeably wider than most windows.

You might have wondered whether what you'd see inside the house or any of the existing homes would be different too, then shrug and think

Townsend, Massachusetts home with solar panels facing south.

maybe not any more than the little you'd seen so far. You'd be right, and that's just the point.

The future of building is not about any radical change in the way houses and other buildings look. It goes deeper, to the way they work, and here the change is nothing short of revolutionary. Put simply, these are houses that will produce as much energy as they use. This balance is summed up in the name they are known by: zero energy or net zero energy homes.

It doesn't stop there, though. The spirit, if not the letter, of zero energy homes requires that the energy produced must be from completely natural renewable energy sources — typically solar, but possibly wind too — converted into electricity on the property. What isn't used at the time it's produced is fed into the local utility grid. Any energy consumed when the sun isn't shining or the wind blowing is also electricity, supplied to the home by traditional fossil fuel-burning power plants. Eventually, however, those plants will be replaced by solar, wind, geothermal and ocean wave power facilities — as they have been in a few communities to some degree today — when coal, oil, propane and natural gas supplies start running out or become more expensive than the renewable sources. (And nuclear facilities become untenable.)

Also, a zero energy home consumes very little energy. The amount should be at least two-thirds, and hopefully as much as ninety percent, less than consumed by a standard house the same size. Smaller houses trump larger too — the better to reduce the amount of energy used.

Inside the house, it's mostly a story about the many ways — small, unseen, out of the way or uncommon — that make up the structure and components of the house that will separate the future from the present and the past. It's a revolution about doing nothing less than changing the way we live — without, as contradictory as it may seem, reinventing the way homes are built. That's because everything it takes to build the house of tomorrow is for sale today, bought off the shelf or from the Internet.

Some of the features and ways of doing things will be new to most homes, though much of what makes up a zero energy house will just be more efficient versions of what's already in them. In the package of features that make up a zero energy home there can be heat or energy recovery ventilator systems, tankless hot water heaters, heat pumps, fiberglass doors, low-flow showerheads, Energy Star top-freezer refrigerators, front-loading clothes washers, LED lighting and cellulose and foam insulation, as well as triple-pane gas-filled windows and solar electric panels.

Finally, a zero energy home *must* be priced within the means of the average homebuyer.

All the houses on Coppersmith Way were built with the goal of reaching zero energy, coming close or at least being far more energy efficient than any standard home. They use many of the features noted above and depend on electricity for nearly all their energy. A few use nothing else and a number of the houses are well below the average house size. (The one house without solar was too close to protected wetlands and the trees there would block the sun from reaching a photovoltaic system.)

Ideally, zero energy homeowners would wind up paying nothing for the electricity they consumed over the course of the year. For the owners of a typical American house, eliminating the entire bill in an all-electric zero energy home could be a savings of about $2,200 annually (2009 figures). It can also mean more money in the pocket later, when the house is sold.

In a study appearing in *The Appraisal Journal,* a home's value was said to increase an average of $20 for each $1 decrease in the annual utility bill.

A higher quality of life — by a number of different measures — is another advantage of living in a zero energy home. The homes are quieter, maintain temperature settings better, allow more natural light, have better air quality and may stand up to storms better than traditional homes. But as welcome as these advantages are, they don't speak to the reason why zero energy homes are — many people would say must be — the housing of the future.

In the United States, buildings, both residential and commercial, account for roughly 40 percent of energy use and carbon emissions, more than either of the other two main sectors of the economy, industry and transportation. Throw in construction and demolition, and it increases to 50 percent.

Governments have seized upon the idea of developing zero energy buildings as a key strategy for cutting down on both energy consumption and pollution as part of worldwide efforts to end global warming. If they are not successful in the next decade or two, it will be fair to question whether there will be a future as we have always thought of it — a time better than what preceded it — for housing or anything else.

New single-family homes have been their prime focus. Existing homes, multifamily residences and industrial and commercial buildings are also targets for efficiency makeovers and on-site solar production, but new single-family homes make a great lead-in. Their impact is relatively small, but they're the easiest to develop and can provide a field lab and a set of standards for all buildings.

This strategy began to take shape in the nineties based on what was already well known. In theory, anyone could build a zero energy building. All it took was enough money to lay out solar panels and/or wind turbines on a property to offset any amount of electricity use. Yet, to do so would likely be beyond the financial reach of most families because of the high cost of solar equipment. Big solar layouts tended to come with big, well-stocked houses that require a lot of energy to run. A family of four in a two-bedroom cottage with a single bathroom and a leaky oil furnace might use less energy than a zero energy home that was larger and didn't maximize energy efficiency.

Another way of developing a zero energy home would be to have a house that was not connected to the grid, which would mean it had to produce all the electricity it used. The problem with those homes, however, was that they were not easily duplicated or desirable in a mostly urban, utility-connected society that over time would need the renewable energy that millions of homes could feed the grid.

They were also of dubious environmental value. They counted on storing electricity in toxic lead acid batteries the size of small refrigerators that would be an eternal nightmare once their useful life was over. (California is looking for ways to use safe lithium-ion batteries, but a cost-effective solution is many years away.)

What was needed instead was, in the words of the US Department of Energy, "marketable zero energy homes"—the kind of zero energy homes that the average American home buyer could shop for on Sunday outings as they would for any other home. It became the job of DOE's Building America program, established in 1995, to make that idea a reality by 2020 and there were soon a few concrete signs. Within five to ten years, a number of private homes that looked much like any other, but that were far more energy efficient and that had solar installations on their roofs were built under the program.

In 2007, California stepped up an aggressive campaign, using tougher and far more encompassing language. The state's Public Utility Commission said in 2008 that "all new residential construction [in California] will be zero net energy by 2020." The European Union chose a variation on the same theme over a similar time frame. In November 2009, its parliament said that, "all buildings built after 31 December 2020 must have high energy saving standards and be powered to a large extent by renewable energy." What "high" and "large" meant was not clear, but it followed a statement that the model for these buildings would be a "near zero energy" standard set for just a year earlier that was required of all new government-sponsored residences. The aims are the same for commercial buildings in Europe and California, only set back to 2030. Japan has a simple one-size-fits-all goal: by 2030 every new building built should be zero energy.

A number of non-profit organizations grew up out of that same nineties environment to promote energy efficiency and sustainable building practices using rating systems. Among the best-known are the US Green Building Council (USGBC), the Residential Energy Services Network (RESNET) and Germany's Passivhaus Institut. They were later joined by many other ratings, rankings and movements, like the American Society of Heating, Refrigerating and Air-Conditioning Engineers' bEQ ratings and German "Triple Zero" designs.

RESNET developed the Home Energy Rating System or HERS, which was a measurement of energy use in comparison to a standard house. For example, a typical new home received a rating of 100, while a zero energy home was 100 percent more efficient and rated, well, 0 (though for years the numbers were reversed).

The USGBC took a somewhat different approach with its Leadership in Energy and Environmental Design (LEED) certification program. This was a measure of sustainable building practices. HERS was a big part of its scoring system, which was an arbitrary point total linked to Olympic-like medal awards.

The Passivhaus Institut went for deep over broad. Builders who maximized the heating and cooling efficiency front end — meaning around 90 percent better than average — would earn its less than scintillating and marketable "quality approved passive house" certification. All other household energy use barely merits a mention and renewable energy sources are not a requirement of the process.

The Washington, DC-based International Code Council (ICC) effectively shortened the distance builders had to travel to reach zero by pushing the starting point forward. Every three years, the ICC meets to raise the building standards for efficiency in its International Energy Conservation Code (IECC). Nearly every state has adopted at least one version. Again, the first one came out in the nineties.

The Federal government, state and local governments and utilities offered financial incentives for making new and existing buildings more energy efficient and for installing solar installations. Depending on where a building owner lived they could get tax credits, low-interest loans, rebates or all of the above.

By the end of the first decade of the 21st century, the various initiatives appeared to be having some impact. Builders scattered about the country began showing an interest in developing the kind of zero energy-rated production homes that might serve as models for large-scale development. Most of them were smaller developers, like Transformations Inc., the developer of the Townsend, Massachusetts, development, but their numbers were growing. Plans were in development, on the drawing boards or in the construction stage from Connecticut to Colorado.

In the next decade the largest home builders started to catch on. KB Home, ranked fifth, and Meritage Homes, number eleven, both laid claim to having built zero energy-rated production homes and promised to build whole developments that — at the request of buyers willing to pay more — could be upgraded to zero energy. Finally, zero energy was slipping into the mainstream. However, more still has to be done. Many more zero energy homes need to be built and they have to prove they can literally produce as much energy as they use year on end. So far, homes that don't receive utility bills appear to be in short supply.

In 2006, the Northeast Sustainable Energy Association (NESEA) created a contest — no cost to enter — to award $10,000 to a home in its 10-state region that qualified as having 12 months of utility bills that added up to zero. It wasn't until three years later that the Massachusetts-based environmental organization found a winner and it was a custom-built home bigger and costing twice as much as the median US house. In the next two annual contests — 2010 and 2011 — there were a total of just ten entries, mostly custom-built, expensive and loaded with solar power.

To be sure, there was also a lot of ground to cover in the century's second decade. A few statistics put the task in perspective. There were 130 million residences in the US in 2009. Single-family homes accounted for 90 million of them, including 7 million attached houses. Mobile and manufactured homes totaled another nine million. In most years before the Great Recession, more than a million new single-family homes were added to the housing stock.

It would be quite a task, to say the least, to suddenly start building that many new zero energy homes when so few were being built 15 years after goals to make them commonplace were set. After all, though the pieces are not new, putting them together for the greatest cost-effective efficiency is beyond the experience of almost every builder and they would have to make a commitment they've lacked so far to do by 2020 what they haven't done since 1995.

While this was the first time builders showed an interest in moving zero energy homes into the mainstream, it was not the first time they had shown interest in building zero energy homes. Major builders like Pulte, Centex and Shea had taken stabs at building prototype zero energy homes a decade earlier without following through. More energy efficient features worked their way into their homes, but that was the extent of it.

Indeed, few builders of any size have made producing even modestly efficient housing part of their routine. For over a decade, the Department of Energy (DOE) has encouraged the nation's home builders to develop Energy Star homes, which are required to be 15 percent more energy efficient than standard homes. Yet, only one million were built or about five percent of all the homes constructed since the Energy Star home program began in 1995, the same year Building America was started. In 2008, DOE started an Energy Challenge program for builders who would build homes that were 30 percent more efficient than standard, but only several thousands homes were built in the first 3 years of the program.

If builders haven't been enthusiastic, buyers haven't shown much interest either. Indeed, home buyers have not given any thought to reducing energy consumption, much less eliminating its costs. When first-time home buyers responded to a study by the National Association of Home Builders (NAHB) released in January 2008 to list the most important factors in buying a house, they named price, layout and space in that order. When pressed to list all the factors that mattered to them they named the same three, followed by the yard, exteriors and quality. If there was a place for energy efficiency and production the only category that would appear to fit would be "quality" — a distant sixth.

Seasoned buyers don't appear to be any different. They were asked only to list their first three reasons, with no follow-up, but the trend seemed clear. They gave the same responses with a slight switch of order that had layout moving ahead of price.

Some experts might say that if pressed on the quality issue, energy efficiency and production still wouldn't make it onto buyers' wish lists. In a lecture Nobel-prize winning physicist Steven Chu gave in 2008, midway between the NAHB study's release and his appointment as Secretary of Energy, he said that new houses could be made more efficient with an investment of $1,000, but that "American consumers would rather have a granite countertop."

Nor would an appeal to their concern for the environment do any better. At least that's the view of some of the wittier observers of social mores, the creators of *The Simpsons*. In *The Simpsons Movie*, when Green Day announces it wants to say a word about "the environment" (after just giving a three-and-a-half-hour performance), they get stoned by the audience, then sink into a toxic sludge while playing the music played when the Titanic went down. Since then — in polls from November 2008 to May 2011 — fewer Americans believe that global warming is occurring. Even among those that do, fewer are sure of it and less than half believe that humans are responsible for it.

Money — or rather the lack of interest in spending it on energy efficiency and renewable energy — is at the heart of the challenge of building zero energy homes. They cost more up front. How much more depends on a number of factors, including the square footage of the home, but about 25 percent more to achieve a zero energy rating is not unusual. Since home buyers in the NAHB study rated price as the most or second most important consideration, zero energy homes start at a huge disadvantage.

The alternative is to build smaller homes so as to reduce the total cost. However, builders love space. It costs relatively little to add, but allows them to increase the home's price and their customers want the extra room. As the third most important factor in home buying, builders have been adding space to homes prodigiously for decades. The median size of the American home was just 1,525 square feet in 1972. Thirty-seven years later it was 2,135 square feet.

This increase doesn't fit with what has been happening to the size of American households, which have been undergoing steady downsizing. There were 3.7 residents in 1940, 3.1 in 1970 and just 2.5 in 2010, so as much as homes have grown, the amount of space individuals have to themselves has increased even more. They each have 854 square feet now compared to about 492 square feet 36 years ago — a staggering gain of more than 70 percent.

Buyers are also unlikely to find in zero energy homes the ideal layout to fit their particular needs. Zero energy homes are laid out with energy efficiency in mind, not the way buyers envision rooms being arranged to match their tastes. Most of the living space and windows, for example, should face south in most parts of the country to make the most of the sun's heat and light. Of course, by virtue of the law of averages there will be some perfect matches. Residents on the south shore of Long Island provide one such example. Their homes contain banks of windows facing the Atlantic south to the horizon, while far fewer windows look out to the noisy traffic along the road on their north side and neighbors east and west. However, across the island to the Gatsby-era estates of the north shore, homeowners would be unlikely to see any wisdom in zero energy design and well they shouldn't. Their homes offer panoramic views facing north along Long Island Sound.

While the two nearby shores may represent extremes, builders throughout the country will generally be caught somewhere in the middle, unable or unwilling to make the best use of the sun. Shade from trees, hills or buildings coming from any direction or unattractive views on their south sides may provide them with good excuses too.

Thomas Siebel, a billionaire Silicon Valley philanthropist, recognized the dilemma of building zero energy homes that could be sold at the same price as the traditional single-family home. In February 2009 he announced that he would award $20 million in prize money to find a solution to the problem. The Energy Free Home Challenge, as he called it, had two stages, both open to anyone in the world. In the first stage anyone who came up with the best technology that would make a marketable zero energy home possible would receive $5 million. In the second stage, ten finalists would be chosen to build zero energy homes, with this new technology at their service. They would each be given $250,000 in prize money and another $250,000 to build a 3-bedroom, 2-bath, 2,000 square-foot house. That month the average price of a new home was $258,600, while the median was $209,700. The homes also had to be built in the same northern locale, probably on land near the campus of the University of Illinois (Siebel's alma mater), necessitating both heating and air-conditioning.

The winner would take home a grand prize of $10 million. It was expected to take about five years to crown a winner, but just as the contest was ready to get underway in the summer of 2009, Siebel was stomped by an elephant in the Serengeti Plain of Tanzania. The challenge was post-poned "indefinitely." his foundation said, while he endured 16 operations on his leg over the next year.

Siebel hoped to make a full recovery. The challenge of developing a zero energy home at the same cost as a conventional house remains and, in fact, has become even more challenging. The world's love of all things that run on electricity has only grown with time. In the first half of electricity's first century in American homes, lighting, radios and refrigerators were the only significant users. In the post-war era, there was an explosion of electric appliances and gadgetry. Television, clothes washers and dryers, dishwashers, air-conditioning, ranges, microwaves, computers, video game sets, DVD players, cell phones and innumerable electric gadgets, including electric blankets, tooth brushes, hair dryers, can openers, exercise equipment, char-gers, iPods and e-books became fixtures in the homes of developed nations. Many were always on, sucking "phantom" energy as if through a straw.

It's no wonder then that residential electricity use had grown to 1,379 billion kilowatt hours annually in 2008 from 67 billion kilowatt hours annually in 1949, according to the Energy Information Administration (EIA), far outstripping the growth of the population. (The numbers are virtually the same for commercial electric consumption.) In recent decades the rate of growth has slowed considerably, but the outlook for cutting back on our energy use isn't encouraging. Whatever timelines governments may impose, the EIA doesn't see any reduction in residential energy use — nor in commercial, transportation or industrial — out to 2035.

Still, that doesn't mean there can't be a dramatic drop in residential energy use. Evidence suggests that incentives are an important engine for change. Solar electric use, for example, is highest in those states that have them and lowest in those that don't. Six of the top ten solar markets listed by the Interstate Renewable Energy Council have among the best financial incentives, including number one California which also has abundant sun-shine. The remaining four are western states with plenty of the latter and space for utilities to develop large-scale solar panel fields.

Lew Pratsch, a former zero energy homes project manager in the Building America program, thinks it's just a matter of moving enough money around. "If you increase the cost of utilities, then used these revenues to provide financial incentives so that homeowners could see it, then it would work," he says. In short, the cost-effectiveness of efficiency and solar production would be obvious and irresistible should the government wield financial carrots and sticks.

Yet, even if zero energy homes remain a major challenge for large-scale development, they will increasingly become the standard by which housing is measured in the developed world.

It's a standard whose meaning is clear virtually everywhere and whereas it can be stretched, it can only be stretched so far. Homeowners who say they live in a zero energy home while paying $100 or $200 a year in utilities are adhering to the spirit if not the letter of zero energy. There's no living up to the spirit of a "green," "efficient," "sustainable" or "eco-friendly" home since there's no standard or benchmark for any of these — certainly, not the high, exact standard of zero — that means the same thing to everyone. Builders toss "green" around with impunity for adding a few good features, like Energy Star appliances, that modestly improve a home's efficiency.

Even the word "zero" or one of its common English synonyms is the same throughout the developed word. For example, it's pronounced and spelled "zero" or close in France, Spain, Italy and Poland.

As ideas travel around the world, zero energy homes will become increasingly accessible to builders and homeowners committed to developing and living in one. In fact, with the passage of time they will be proven to be cheaper than traditional homes. That's because owners who stay in them over the length of a typical mortgage will get a return on their investment through energy savings far greater than with any other housing.

Not that the obstacles facing large-scale development prevent individuals from developing their own zero energy homes now. They merely need a willingness to be open to something new and different. Where and how the house is built, by whom and with what and how it's financed — all concerns for building any home — will require a fresh perspective.

At this stage in the history of zero energy, prospective developers will have to be pioneers. Builders will be self-taught and home buyers will have to take on the role of general contractor. This in itself is not an unusual role for home buyers to be in. Enough information is available so that there need be no mystery to developing a house that is extremely efficient and produces as much energy as needed at a price middle-class buyers can afford. Production information, builders and even designs are a click away. Attics loaded with insulation are readily obtained. Low-flow plumbing fixtures' time has come. The advantages of buying the most efficient type of mass-produced refrigerator should be indisputable. More than a few tasks should be routine, cost effective and supremely satisfying.

It will take some adjustments. Size will likely have to be scaled back and there has been some scaling back by builders. Compromises in layouts may be needed, though moving exposure to sunlight up the wish list should be easy to accept. Behavior may also need to be modified. The neighbors will probably have more electronic gadgetry and hands need to be seen as the useful substitute they are. Zero energy will need to be seen as "cool" the way giving up smoking became a goal worthy of the effort. This will come, many behavioral scientists and economists think, when enough Jones's live in zero energy homes and many others will strive to keep up with them.

Not that the homeowner or buyer has to go all the way all at once, or ever. While the aim is to hit zero, anyone taking on the job can pull up short or pick and choose what they want to do knowing that no more than a handful of builders have even gotten halfway there. Given the low risk of failing to beat the pack, there's no better place to start than the beginning with nothing or, rather, zero to lose.

Following the Sun

T HE TWO-STORY HOME ON THE SOUTH SIDE of a straight flat stretch on a road outside of Urbana, Illinois, appears to be as much a part of its rural environment as the ground surrounding it. Large stone bases support beams holding up a porch roof at the front and eastern and western sides of the house. The siding is a combination of earth tones. A three-foot high strip of brown gives way to the brownish-gray color of the roof. Its sharp square shape and low gabled roof gives the home a solid imposing look of midwestern permanence.

Yet while it seems, like many homes in its area, to have been planted on its foundation and been quietly blending into its surroundings for a long time, that image is deceiving. This Urbana home was completed in 2008 and its shell or envelope is not just standing there, but is very busy reducing the amount of energy needed to run the home.

This work is done just by the way the home is designed and built, a concept known as passive design. The idea is that by incorporating a few relatively simple features into the house it will make the most — and, when wanted, the least — of the sun's energy. Passive design succeeds best when it allows as much of the sun's heat in as possible through its windows

GREGORY STANTON

Outside of Urbana, Illinois, facing north (right) and east.

during cold months and keeps it out in hot months. Good passive design also allows sunlight in through the windows, while keeping the wind from penetrating the seams around them or anywhere else in the house's structure all year round.

Letting the sun through the home's windows in the winter means a homeowner can bask in its warmth and natural light while paying smaller utility bills. Keeping it from shining through the windows in the summer means the cost of running air-conditioning systems will be less.

Passive design could just as easily be called simple design. Its focus is on not complicating a few mostly basic features common to all buildings. These include orientation, shape, size, insulation, windows, doors, ventilation and landscaping. There are no moving parts to contend with, except with ventilation and, to a lesser extent, windows.

Good passive design is desirable throughout most of the country because the sun's heat and light can contribute to energy efficiency almost everywhere. Where there isn't much of a need, if any, for its heat indoors, as in the Deep South and parts of the Southwest where cooling predominates, developers may decide in favor of having little or no direct sunlight in the house all year long.

The Right Spot

Passive design begins with site selection. Ideally, it's best to have a site where the southern boundaries of the property are unobstructed and the entrance to the home will be on the eastern, western or northern side.

The light from the sun entering Earth's atmosphere spends most of its time in the northern hemisphere shining on the southern face of anything it strikes. An unobstructed window facing that direction — plus or minus 20 degrees, which at the greatest deviation will still provide 92 percent of the sun's heat facing due south — allows more of the sun's energy to pass through during the course of the day than a similar window located on any of the house's other sides. (In the southern hemisphere it's north-facing windows that do best.)

The ideal however, is as rare a commodity for zero energy homes as it is with most things in life. Roughly speaking, less than 25 percent of home sites qualify.

Take a typical housing development, the kind built by major home-building companies that are laid out on vast tracts of land in grid-like formation. The classic example is Levittown, New York, built between 1947 and 1951. More than half a century later the tradition of building large planned communities continues. The top ten builders in the US, which includes D.R. Horton, Lennar, Pulte and Centex, alone build 25 percent of all new homes and that percentage is expected to rise to 33 percent in the coming decades.

Mass producing homes laid out on a grid leads to the same exposures repeated time and again. The grid may not be obvious from the ground level. It may be rectangular, irregular or both, like the planned community built by D.R. Horton in Windsor, Colorado, or the one built by Lennar in Waretown, New Jersey, but several left or right turns will quickly bring a driver back to where they started.

For example, think of the streets in one of these communities that run north and south. The homes will generally have their windows facing east and west, to the street and the backyard, with few windows looking out on their neighbors on the north and south sides. The other two streets in the grid — the ones running east and west — will have just the opposite arrangement. Most of their window area will face north and south. That gives both the potential for maximizing the southern exposure, but only those on the north end are, for all practical purposes, in a position to realize it. Their south sides — the backyard — are not going to have entrances or garages taking up potential window space and they offer better privacy for bedrooms and living rooms, which get the most window area.

If the grid is square, then 25 percent of the homes will likely have the ideal. If it's a rectangle, it would be more or less than 25 percent, depending on whether the length of the grid runs north and south (less) or east and west (more).

While facing a core of backyards may be the most common way to secure an open southern exposure throughout urban and suburban tracts of homes, it's not the only way. Move up the economic ladder and builders can utilize strategies to orient more homes to the south by developing cul du sacs. This way, the entrance road and the homes can be arranged so as to give the homes a southern exposure while also endowing them with a bit of individuality and perhaps more privacy.

Sometimes though, nothing will work. Tall buildings, trees and hills or mountains can stand in the way of the southern exposure. There are also times when no matter how open a site is to southern exposures no one could be blamed for ignoring it. This could be the northern developer who opens his homes to beautiful vistas of mountains, lakes or urban skylines to the north — braving its brutal winter winds — while turning the back side of their houses, where they install garages and utility rooms, over to highways, shopping malls and other developments. More simply, the southern exposure just may come at too high a price for reasons that may or may not have anything to do with its exposure.

THE INFILL EXCEPTION

There are times when even a southern exposure, even one with a great view and an affordable price, should be turned down. This could be the case when the choice is between developing virgin land or an infill. The main difference between the two is that in the former the land hasn't been developed while the latter has been at one time or another. An infill may be a site where a house burned down, or is abandoned or condemned. An infill might be created when a homeowner puts a piece of their property up for sale or an oddly shaped vacant lot between two developments becomes available. Yet another is when a commercial or industrial lot gets zoned for housing. The US Census began tracking density for the first time in the 2000 Census, signaling a growing interest in managing land use better.

What unites infills is that developing them will be more energy efficient than opening up virgin land for a variety of reasons. No energy will likely be expended preparing the land for development because it was likely to have been leveled before. Water, sewage and gas and electric utilities will probably all be in place or reasonably accessible. Public transportation, shopping, entertainment and schools will generally be nearby.

The decades-long decline of inner cities in the Rust Belt where boarded-up homes, closed factories and vacant lots are common provides opportunities for developing infills. More recently, the collapse of the speculative housing market in 2008 that left developments unfinished — with capped sewer connections sticking up out of the ground — has extended the potential for developing infills to other parts of the country.

Virgin land however, will take a lot of energy to develop and there's less of it with each passing year. A stand of trees may have to be cleared for nothing better than kindling which means it will literally be going up in smoke, thereby adding carbon emissions to the atmosphere. A septic tank and well will probably have to be installed and electric utility lines will have to be brought in, increasing the burden on existing systems. The homeowner will also expend more energy living there. Further away from most places they want to reach, they will be spending more time burning fossil fuel by driving to wherever they need to go.

No Southern Exposure; No Problem

In the end, home builders can't count on southern exposure as much as they'd like and not having it means looking for significant energy savings and production elsewhere. Virtually nowhere in Germany or Austria are there vast tracts of open space available for building single-family homes, and finding a perfect southern exposure is many, many times more difficult than in the United States or Canada. European countries also receive far less sunlight than most of the US or Canada. Yet, Germany and Austria have literally thousands of passive design homes built since the late nineties that use as much as 90 percent less energy in heating and cooling than the average home. Germany also has far more solar capacity than does the United States.

Germany is able to do it because orientation is just one facet of passive design. Some sacrifice or compromise may be required elsewhere in the building process without the perfect southern exposure, but that's exactly how zero energy homes are developed. Give a little here; get some somewhere else.

The Shape of Things To Come

The best shape for a zero energy house is the simplest construction with sides, and that is a cube. If that's too simple for builders and buyers then it should, at least, be a rectangular prism whose length is only slightly longer than its width. It's a mathematical certainty that the cube is the most efficient and least costly shape.

The proof is in equations using calculus or algebra, but throwing out a few simple arithmetic examples may drive the point home more clearly. Start with a square with a side of any length. Stretch it out into a rectangle with the same area. The difference is in the perimeter. The rectangle's is greater.

For example, a square with an area of 36 square feet has sides of 6 feet long and a perimeter of 24 feet. The rectangle with the same area and closest whole number dimensions is 9 feet by 4 feet with a perimeter of 26 feet. Stretching it out some more — 12 feet by 3 feet — results in a sum of 30 feet and one more time — 18 feet by 2 feet — leads to a perimeter of 40 feet.

The longer the rectangle (and a square is just a special kind of rectangle), the larger the perimeter. These are not just numbers, either, when it comes to living space. The longer the house and the further it deviates from a square, the more materials a builder will need for the same space. Increase the number of sides and material needs increase even more. All this adds to the cost of the home.

It gets more expensive when considering what the extra money is being spent on. The simplest way of seeing this is by turning a two-story home in the shape of a cube into a one-story home that is now a rectangular prism with the same volume. The rising costs are not just due to buying more of the same, but in spending the money differently. The two-story home has the added expense of a staircase and a second floor, but having to spend more on siding, framing, foundation, insulation and roofing for the single-story home is going to cost significantly more.

A home that is not a cube will also be less energy efficient. Heat has more opportunity to escape in the winter and penetrate in the summer because there is more surface area for the same amount of interior space and a greater total distance over which sides meet sides, roof and foundation. Plumbing and ventilating lines will be longer — and more costly — in single-story homes than two. The combination of vertical and horizontal lines in a two-story house will be less than the strictly horizontal lines in a single-story home. It's worth adding that with a boxier two-story home it is easier to centralize lines than it is with a long rectangular home with the same space. The advantage is having fewer lines extending to far-off corners of the home — and lower costs yet.

Two-story homes have been gaining in popularity over the last forty years and account for over half of new homes. However, there will always be buyers who will want to live without climbing stairs and, with an aging population, more won't be able to make the effort. It wouldn't be too surprising if the two-story trend goes into reverse in coming decades.

One way of developing two-story homes with single-story living is to have the master bedroom on the first floor. The second floor's value is then to maintain a broad marketing appeal should there come a time to sell the house, and to provide room for visiting adult children, grandchildren and other guests.

Finally, the cube's simplicity helps reduce cost yet another way, by keeping design costs to a minimum, if not eliminating them all together. This is as it should be, according to Matthew O'Malia, an architect who developed a home in rural Belfast, Maine, shaped as a cube (with the obligatory New England mud room attached). It is one of the few passive houses in the United States recognized by the Passive House Institute US. It also has solar panels and is nearly a zero energy home too. "You've got to eliminate the cost of an architect," he says. "Otherwise, you can't afford to build and sell a zero energy home at a reasonable price and still make a profit."

Eliminating architects for all but the more expensive homes can be challenging (though not impossible considering that during 2010 one industry estimate put architect unemployment at upwards of 13 percent). The grander the home, the more admired — and energy inefficient — it tends to be, even more so when it comes to shape. The Palace of Versailles is roughly in the shape of an "X" with the forward slash about five times as long as it is wide, while the backslash more than twice as long as it is wide. No side faces south either. The White House is better, but still on the wrong side of efficiency. It's more than twice as long as it is wide, though it does face south.

Nevertheless, there are enough styles that lend themselves to zero energy development and are right for every environment. Colonial, adobe, contemporary and modern designs are often enough little more than cubes. The four hundred-year-old saltbox design provides an excellent match for zero energy development and one very specific home style virtually anticipated zero energy homes when it first appeared on the scene a hundred years ago. It's the American Foursquare design, which is little more than a cube with a porch. Similar to that is the two-story passive house with the Frank Lloyd Wright prairie influence and southern exposure that is owned by a retired couple outside of Urbana, Illinois — ironically, a stone's throw away from the area Thomas Siebel was considering for his zero energy challenge contest.

Size Counts

Size is another facet of passive design, if not the single most important one. The median-size home in the first decade of the 21st century in the US cannot be made into a zero energy home for the same cost as the median price new home. In 2009, the median size home was 2,135 square feet; the median price home cost $216,700. (Median size means that half of all the homes built in the US that year were larger and half were smaller; median price means that half were more expensive and half cheaper.)

It may have been possible to build a 1,500 square foot home for the median price that year, though even that size might be overly generous.

David Pill, a Vermont architect who built and lives in the first NESEA zero energy winner, thinks 1,300 square feet, about half the size of his home, is a good bet.

His estimate is in line with a number of noteworthy zero energy projects. The winner of the 2010 NESEA award and also the winner of the first and only Massachusetts Zero Energy Challenge, the first statewide competition in the country, was 1,152 square feet. The runner-up in the Massachusetts contest was 1,252 square feet. Both received below zero energy HERS ratings, while the third place finisher narrowly missed touching bottom. It was 1,392 square feet.

Several other small examples can be found across the country. In another part of Urbana stands the first passive house in the US, which is just 1,200 square feet. In Edmond, Oklahoma, Ideal Homes built what it billed as the first zero energy production home for under $200,000, in 2006. It's 1,650 square feet and came up short of zero by about a third when actual energy use exceeded projections during its first year of occupancy.

In Colorado, the first zero energy home built by Habitat for Humanity, which builds homes to sell to low-income families, has a floor space of 1,280 square feet and went beyond zero, producing more energy than it uses.

Mass producing zero energy homes could allow builders like Ideal to realize economies of scale and build homes closer in size to the median that achieve zero energy at the same cost. Sticking to a standard design rather than changing it is worth, says Vernon McKown, Ideal's co-owner and president of sales, a savings of ten percent. True zero energy designs are not likely to become standard until government and most home builders and buyers start thinking smaller. A 3,000 square foot zero energy home is or should become an oxymoron.

Scaling down shouldn't be an insurmountable goal. Americans lived smaller a generation ago and home sizes have through 2010 remained below both their median and average peak, set in 2007. A 2010 survey by the American Institute of Architects found that 57 percent of architecture firms reported a decrease in the square footage in the homes they were working on compared to 13 percent 5 years earlier. Moreover, a significant segment of the population in all developed countries already live well with considerably less space than is found in typical homes. Many of them are affluent too. They also may pay far more for their residences than even owners of the biggest McMansions do.

They're apartment dwellers. They occupy more than ten percent of all US residences, and according to the 2000 Census, their apartments average less than half the space found in the median-sized single family home.

Seeing The Light

The homes at 5652 Woodwind Hills Drive and 2663 Woodwind Hills Lane in Lakeland, Florida, are the exact same size and shape and both face

The Lakeland, Florida twin (front and back) that was built with the aim of reaching zero energy.

south. The sites are virtually identical, too, as the houses are in a line (on either side of a third house) separated by only two hundred feet over open, flat land.

There is however, one difference in their physical structure and it literally sticks out. The first home's roof extends three feet rather than one and a half feet out from the walls of the house. While hardly noticeable, the effect on energy usage is significant. The home with the broader overhang uses seven percent less electricity than its twin.

Selecting the site, orienting the home and determining its shape, structure and size is only the set-up for how passive designs control the sun's heat and light. The job itself is left to the windows. The kind they are, their size, where they are located and any pairing with thermal mass and overhangs will determine to a significant degree how much heat and light gets inside.

Windows are not part of the shell's construction. They are separate factory-built goods shipped to the site and installed into the envelope. The spaces left for them and any overhangs and thermal masses associated with windows are, however, integral parts of the shell. Windows and doors will get their own chapter, while their place in the envelope is covered here.

From caves to igloos to tepees to yurts to geodesic domes, humans have shown that they can live without windows. Homes without them are cheaper to build and more energy efficient than homes with windows. There are other advantages too, such as no glass to wash and no worries over peeping Toms or baseballs shattering glass.

Buckminster Fuller became famous for his geodesic dome designs, but not rich, and therein lies the rub. Homeowners like windows and like to have plenty of them in their homes. The trick is to satisfy the need to look out and let some light in without making it too difficult to reach zero energy.

Basic passive design in zero energy homes calls for window area equaling about 12 percent of the house's floor space. For example, a 1,500 square foot home would have 180 square feet of windows. The south side of the home should get about 7 of the 12 percentage points. The north would get about four, while east and west together would get the rest, which is to say almost nothing. Follow the numbers this far and the task of achieving zero energy is on track.

Still, more could be done, all on the south side. Window space may be increased and heat-absorbing material added, as well as overhangs.

All the work on the south side is to control the sun's heat and light. The north-facing windows provide indirect light to the other side of the house. They don't get as much space as the south side since they open the house in most climates to winter's cold winds. The east and west are largely ignored because they will likely provide too much direct heat in the summer for anyone outside the coldest climates without filling any real natural lighting needs not already adequately provided for by the other two sides.

Overhangs are used to protect the inside of the house from too much of the sun's heat. They do it by extending far enough out to block the sun's rays during the hottest hours of the summer when they're beaming down from high in the sky. But they don't stick out far enough to block the sun in the winter, when it peaks at a lower angle. Builders use a widely accepted and simple formula based entirely on a home's latitude to figure out how far the overhang should extend.

Coupling the winter sun with thermal mass inside the house is a way of sucking more free heat out of the sun. The thermal mass, a technical term for heat-absorbing material like certain floor tiles or just plain concrete floors, acts as storage for the extra heat, which is released inside at night.

Building a Trombe wall into the home's south face is a way of passively maximizing heat gain. This may be thought of as cutting a slab of the thermal mass out of the floor and making it stand up against a framed sheet of glass its exact size to serve much the same purpose as when it was lying down.

Smart Compromises

Following the north/south-east/west formula may actually work out for reasons having nothing to do with energy efficiency. A buyer of a house in a large development sandwiched between east and west neighbors may welcome solid walls in those directions for privacy reasons and think the extra energy efficiency a bonus. The shade provided by overhangs may also provide a measure of privacy as well solar protection. Then again they may not work out. They may be seen as too great a departure from what buyers and builders expect to see in a mainstream house.

That was true for Carter Scott. He was the builder of the second-place finisher in the Massachusetts Zero Energy Challenge. His house had the entrance on the west, with the garage on the north, and when asked why he had given considerable space to windows surrounding the entrance, he said, "I want to sell houses."

If zero energy pioneers have to make choices favoring conventional over passive design, it only shows that any hopes of mainstreaming passive design may depend on being flexible.

The Trombe wall, for one, seems an easy sacrifice. For starters, it doesn't obey a cardinal tenet of building zero energy homes. It's not something that can be bought off the shelf, and with its foreboding appearance, like the iconic black slab in the science fiction classic, *2001,* it may never be. Indeed, Trombe walls may be one of the few useful products left in the world without even a dedicated online organization — National Association of Trombe Wall Builders? — promoting them and listing contractors who can build them.

Overhangs might also be dropped — at least halfway. While roofs that stick out further than most may find wide acceptance, an overhang jutting out over first floor windows on one side of a two-story house might look too much like the appendage it is to find a wide audience.

Loading up the south face with windows and leaving little for the other three faces presents a natural lighting problem for bedrooms. For decades the traditional home has had three bedrooms and it would be difficult for all three to share the sunny south side. One is likely to be left in the cold and dark with indirect light from a window the size of a ship's portal — an arrangement few families of four would find advantageous.

Passive design for windows may also have limited use because of costs. The upfront expense may be too much for builders and buyers to wrap their minds around when the payback — energy savings — are too slow in coming. This may be particularly true when giving up to 12 percent or more of floor space to windows. Windows can be one of the most expensive parts of any home, especially if they're highly energy efficient. There's truly more to them than meets the eye. Super-efficient windows are more akin to heating and lighting control systems than framed glass and it's a lot cheaper to fill the space with siding, framing, insulation and paint.

Loading up on window space may not even make the home more energy efficient and could easily make it less efficient. The quickest way for heat to get into the house in summer and out in winter is through the windows.

It should then come as no surprise that coming up short on passive design efficiency doesn't mean zero energy at a reasonable cost is out of reach. The homes built by Carter Scott came close to zero without being faithful to passively designed windows.

Growing Energy Efficiency

In satirizing postwar suburban conformity, folk singer Malvina Reynolds memorably reduced the homes to "little boxes all the same." Before extending the line to zero energy homes, consider one other aspect of passive design that makes the zero energy home environment more attractive, while improving the house's energy efficiency.

Planting trees and other forms of landscaping can soften the edges of zero energy homes while protecting them and their owners from summer's heat and winter's cold. Fresher air and enhanced privacy are bonuses, as well as the general good feeling that comes from planting trees as rainforests are being decimated. If those reasons aren't enough to extend passive design to landscaping, here's one more: it's free, or very close to it. Most if not all the trees and shrubs can be ordered from non-profit organizations for nothing or by paying a small charge for shipping or membership in the organization.

What trees and shrubs work best depends on where a home is located. Where they're planted around the house is also important. Get both right and they'll provide insulation for a home all year round.

Spruce trees are a good choice for the north side of the house. They'll act as windbreakers to reduce the amount of cold air penetrating a home in winter, reducing heating needs. For the best protection, the spruces should be located a distance from a house of from two to five times the mature height of the trees.

Planting deciduous trees along the west side of a house provides shading that will protect it from the late afternoon summer sun. That way the home will be cooler and the air conditioning bill lower because the air conditioner can be set at a lower temperature. Most any local tree that provides good shading will do the job well and shading can reduce air conditioning demand by at least ten percent. In the winter, with the leaves gone, the sun shines in.

Whatever trees are chosen, they shouldn't grow any taller than the house because they'll block the sun's path to solar panels on the roof. An Amur maple is an excellent choice. It's a hardy, spreading tree with a great red color in the autumn. It will grow in most soils to about 20 feet high so it won't block the late day sun from reaching solar panels on a two-story roof. Urban Forestry divides trees by height: under and above 30 feet tall. (Website addresses of organizations mentioned in the text can be found in the Resources section at the end of the book.)

Among the organizations that will give trees away to anyone anywhere are the Arbor Day Foundation and Free Trees and Plants.Com. The Arbor Day Foundation gives out ten free trees for an annual membership of just $10, while Free Trees requests that shipping fees be paid for.

A better alternative for many homeowners may be state forestry commissions. A number of them sell indigenous trees at modest prices to state residents and will be closer to home for many people. Curiously, both Arbor and Free Trees are in Nebraska and depending on where you live, shipping their trees could involve the release of more carbon emission in the course of shipping than is necessary. Among the states that have forest commissions that sell low-cost seedlings are South Carolina, Georgia, Virginia and Kentucky. The National Association of State Foresters has a complete list of contacts.

The trees you get will depend on availability. If Arbor, Free Trees or a state forestry commission doesn't have the Amur maple it can easily be purchased at many nurseries or online. A two to three foot tree will cost about $28, with shipping and tax. Patience — measured in years — will be its own reward. Seeds are $3 a pack.

Sustainable Passive Design

Passive design doesn't have anything to say about the materials used to build the shell. Nor will the choice of wood for framing, the type of roofing and driveway and the materials used for siding and foundations really have anything to do with reaching zero. Yet some choices are more in keeping with the spirit of zero energy than others. They are sustainable where others are not and take less energy to produce.

Framing

It has the logo of a tree's outline ending in a check mark: Forest Stewardship Council (FSC) wood isn't a brand, but a promise that the forests the wood comes from are sustainable. It should be the wood of choice for zero energy homes. Still, for the foreseeable future it probably will work only for larger budgets. FSC-sanctioned wood costs more than comparable wood that is not FSC harvested. Scouting prices online and calls to dealers who sell both turned up differences of from 10 to 30 percent.

A zero energy home also may use *more* wood, of any kind, than a conventional home the same size and shape. The framing tends to be wider — at least 2x6-inch lumber versus 2x4-inch — to accommodate more insulation. Also, walls should be extended into the attic rather than having the roof meet the ceiling to allow for as much insulation at the edges of the attic as at the center. (Fewer boards are used — every 24 inches instead of every 16 — to accommodate more insulation, but fewer of wider can still be more costly.)

It will help keep framing costs in check if roof trusses are factory-made, as is the case with most production home builders. They're stronger, as well as cheaper. Staircases can also be factory built. The simplest and cheapest are box stairs, which are straight and have walls on both sides.

Still, framing a single zero energy home with FSC wood may wind up costing thousands of dollars more. Shopping around might reduce the difference or even possibly eliminate it, but doing so presents another hurdle to overcome for building with FSC wood. Only about five percent of North American forests, which provides most of the lumber used in US homes, is certified by the FSC. What that means for builders and buyers alike is that while both small and large lumber outlets carry it, FSC wood is not widely available and the yards where it is stocked may not have what the buyer wants. If they do, they may not be prepared to ship it or the cost could be prohibitive.

Efforts to track down some at Home Depot are instructive. The retailer plainly refers to FSC wood as one of its "Eco-Options" on its website, but calls to stores across the country uncovered mixed results. At branches in New York and Vermont, clerks did not have any in stock and, in fact, did not know what it was, while a Los Angeles outlet had only some FSC plywood.

Determined FSC buyers would do well to start their search for sellers with the FSC website, which is by no means limited to lumber and includes many other wood products. A compromise might be to stick with North American wood over wood from developing countries in Asia. The Asian wood may be cheaper, like common lauan plywood, but it might have been harvested from rainforests that were destroyed through clear-cutting.

SIDING

Fiber cement can be one of the best looking, most sustainable and inexpensive features of zero energy homes. It's currently only in fourth place among sidings used in building new homes, behind vinyl, brick and stucco, but it's gaining on second and third, after not even being tracked by the US Census until 2005.

The siding's increasing popularity is well deserved. Fiber cement is durable, non-toxic, widely available and cheaper than most of the competition. It also holds paint well. Brick and stucco are not even in the race for middle-class dollars. While both are excellent sidings, they cost more than fiber cement and fall outside the budgets for the majority of new homes since the nineties.

Vinyl is really the only serious competition for zero energy home siding dollars and it loses in just about every category. Fiber cement lasts about 50 years — longer than most vinyl siding material. Fiber cement is made of natural material — 45 percent each of Portland cement and sand plus 10 percent wood fiber — whereas vinyl is made of polyvinyl chloride (PVC), a toxic compound after its useful life is over. So fiber cement presents no problems when it's time for new siding. It may wind up in a landfill, but it will do no harm and can actually be recycled as road fill.

Vinyl's afterlife, however, may cause serious health risks — skin lesions and, possibly, cancer — because of dioxin emissions from the PVC. There's little potential for recycling, which means the dioxin gets in the soil when dumped or in the air when burned.

Fiber cement siding.

CERTAINTEED CORP.

Fiber cement can be spruced up during its long life because it can be painted. With vinyl, there's no painting, just the color the siding came as, though it has to be cleaned from time to time.

Where vinyl comes out on top is price. R.S. Means, a popular construction cost source, says fiber cement will cost about 50 percent more or about $3 a square foot compared to about $2 a square foot for vinyl. The cost for both includes material and labor, but the fiber cement siding has more of both because of the paint and painting involved. With its price disadvantage relative to vinyl, fiber cement has its work cut as a choice for home cladding in general and for zero energy homes in particular. With so many features of zero energy houses putting financial pressures on budgets that don't exist with ordinary homes, builders and buyers might have a difficult time deciding in its favor when there are no energy savings. The hope for fiber cement is that if it continues to become more popular the price difference with vinyl may come down and give it a better shot at finding its way into zero energy budgets.

ROOFING

Roofing is another two-horse race in a field of five with the more expensive and sustainable entry the preferred candidate, where zero energy developers can afford it. Steel is the sustainable choice over asphalt, which dominates the market with an 80 percent share. Tile, slate and wood are the budget-busting also-rans. Good looks help account for their higher costs, so hiding them under solar panels, especially the traditionally light-colored tile and wood roofs, would be self-defeating.

Once again the zero energy favorite is the more durable, safer and sustainable pick. Steel will easily outlast asphalt. Manufacturers typically guarantee 50 years and there seems to be little doubt that it can last much longer, while asphalt is surely going to need replacement before the steel gives out. Another advantage steel has over asphalt is that so much of it is recycled. More than half of the steel used in roofs is recycled, while some ten out of eleven million tons of asphalt shingles wind up in landfills annually.

Steel roofs are also lighter, stronger and offer more peace of mind in case of fire. They are fireproof, while asphalt shingles are only fire resistant — to a greater or lesser degree depending on the shingles, which are graded A to C, best to least. Whatever the difference in fire damage between asphalt and steel, homeowners with steel roofs earn a discount on fire insurance.

However, for all its advantages, steel isn't a compelling pick over asphalt the way fiber cement tops vinyl. Asphalt is not nearly the horror vinyl is. While dirty enough, with oil making up one-third of the compound, it's not laden with toxins the way vinyl is. Asphalt's recycling picture is more upbeat than vinyl's too. In recent years a whole network of asphalt shingle recycling alternatives have sprung up and it can actually be cheaper to recycle asphalt shingles than to dump them. Ideal Recycling of Southfield, Michigan, for example, has the capacity to recycle 52,000 tons of shingles per year. It charges $18 to $20 a ton or less than what local landfills would charge for dumping the shingles. (The shingles are then used in paving roads and making new shingles, though these are much more expensive than the originals — or steel). Recyclers can be found through the Construction Material Recycling Association.

The durability issue isn't as clear either. Some asphalt shingles last longer than others. There are two types of asphalt shingles: fiberglass and

Steel panel roof.

IDEAL ROOFING AND THE METAL ROOFING ALLIANCE

organic. Fiberglass asphalt shingles are the more widely used of the two, the most fire resistant and capable of lasting decades.

Still, when all is said and done, asphalt dominates the market the way it does because it's cheap. It may run 25 to 50 percent less than the cost of a steel roof. The hope of narrowing the margin is dependent on oil prices rising faster than those of steel, as they are expected to over time. For the foreseeable future, though, asphalt shingle's low cost may be impossible to ignore. A typical 2,000 square-foot steel roof might easily cost over $10,000, while the same in asphalt will cost several thousand dollars less.

If a budget has room for steel, the best strategy is to buy simple. (New England Metal Roof has a calculator on its web site.) There are basically three categories of steel roof products: shingles (much like asphalt only steel), standard panels (the best-known being corrugated), and standing seam panels. The standard is the cheapest of the three. Among the less expensive standard panels are the 5V Crimp, Royal Lock and Slimline. All use 29 gauge steel. Shingles and standing seam are generally considered more attractive and they will last longer — though any steel roof stands a good chance of outlasting its owner or several of them.

PAINT

One of the areas where sustainability has made the greatest inroads is with paints for covering siding, roofs or interior walls. Big and small paint manufacturers have greatly reduced the level of volatile organic compounds

(VOCs) found in paints, both voluntarily and in response to government regulations.

The VOCs found in paint are not as bad as the PVC in vinyl siding, but they are toxic and pose respiratory and other health risks. Paint is considered low in VOCs if it has below 50 grams of VOCs per liter for flat paint and 150 for non-flat. "Zero" VOCs is actually near-zero or less than five grams per liter for traditional paint. No VOCs are found in natural paints, which may be made from plants, though they are mainstream challenged and likely to stay that way against such dominating and reasonably sustainable competition.

Paint will typically cost anywhere from $10 to $50 a gallon and up. It's not necessarily true that the high-priced paint is five times as good — easier to maintain, longer lasting, more fire resistant and easier to spread over a wide area — as cheaper brands. It is, however, true that low- and zero-VOC paints tend to be priced near the higher end of the range and may be comparable in quality to some high-priced, high-VOC paints.

Low- and zero-VOC paints are becoming widely available in stores and online. Two non-profit organizations, Greenguard and Green Seal, help with the names by providing lists of paints on their websites that are certified low-VOC as well as having other environmental qualities. (Nor are their sites limited to paints.)

Consumer Reports reviewed eight interior low- and zero-VOC paints in 2008 and followed it up with a report on 50 the following year. The most glowing review in their 2009 story went to Home Depot's Behr paints. Says the report: "Behr Premium Plus Ultra paints earned the top spot in the low-luster, flat, and semi-gloss categories we tested and also have less than 50 grams of VOCs per liter. At $31 to $34 per gallon, the Premium Plus Ultra finishes cost more than many other paints we reviewed, though they also have a built-in primer, which could save you time and money if you're painting over bare wood or wallboard."

If the cost of low- and zero-VOC paint puts pressure on a zero energy home budget, a cheaper paint with a higher VOC level could be used on the exterior. However, should covering fiber cement siding with VOC-filled paint sting the conscience, remember it's still less harmful than vinyl siding.

FOUNDATION

Slab-on-grade foundations should be the only foundations for zero energy homes. Foundations are made of concrete and the less used the better because making it requires an incredible amount of energy — more than steel. Concrete manufacturing is responsible for six to eight percent of carbon emissions. Slabs are relatively cheap, too, a good place to save money, and will have no trouble supporting the house. A smaller foundation could reduce labor and equipment costs too. A backhoe is needed to prepare the site for the foundation and they're rented out by the day. A zero energy-sized house might be done in two days. Something larger may take more.

Their drawbacks are relatively minor. It's tougher to access plumbing lines and there's no place for homeowners' junk and teenage rock bands. Fortunately, basements do not appear to be a major issue. More than half of all new homes are already built on slabs of one kind or another, with basements and crawl spaces running second and third, respectively.

Whatever the type of foundation, the amount of cement used in the concrete can be reduced along with energy expenditure and cost. Several strategies work, including shrinking the foundation's size and adding fly ash to the concrete mix. Slabs may be as thin as four inches or as thick as ten inches. A figure closer to the former could be the target given the smaller footprint of a zero energy home. Slabs may also come with feet in cold climates and it's possible to turn these into stubs (frost-protected shallow foundations). How that's done depends on how the foundation is insulated and that will be covered in the chapter on insulation.

Replacing approximately 10 to 30 percent of the Portland cement in concrete with fly ash will use less energy in preparing the mix. Although the cost of fly ash concrete is the same as ordinary concrete, it could be lower in the future since the ash is simply the waste left over from the burning of coal and energy prices are expected to climb. As energy prices climb the cost of producing concrete will rise too and buyers of lite concrete (20 percent fly ash) may save money by choosing it over the traditional kind.

Using the ash for making concrete serves another purpose by recycling the waste instead of dumping it. Fly ash concrete is also stronger and more durable than ordinary concrete. The only serious drawback to fly ash concrete is that it isn't as widely available as traditional concrete, but getting it should be well worth any extra effort.

GARAGE AND DRIVEWAY

At some point early in the history of automobiles homeowners started parking them in the carriage house and the garage was born. It may have once made at least some sense for a car to have its own home. The first cars, like the carriages, were open vehicles and the garages kept them dry in rain and snow and relatively cool in the summer. There may have even been a case for moving the garage into the home, where its owners lived. Homeowners now were able to get to their cars without facing unpleasant weather. They could also avoid their children when they want to be driven to the mall instead of doing their homework since many master bedrooms are closer to the garage than to other bedrooms.

However, garages have no place in zero energy homes or, really, any other home yet to be built. The costs far outweigh any benefits. They at best offer a minor convenience, and, with time, room to store junk that would have otherwise been dumped in a basement. Only now the energy, as well as financial resources needed to build them, are both too much to justify incorporating these drafty, odorous eyesores into the family home.

Builders and buyers are currently light years away from moving their cars outside. Eighty-six percent of new homes have garages, including zero energy-rated homes like those in the Townsend, Massachusetts, development, but there is hope. The percentage of homes without garages has increased to 12 percent from 8 percent during the years 2005 to 2009 and the percentage of three car garages dropped to 17 percent from 20 percent over the same period.

Whatever the reason for the increase in auto homelessness, garages tend to be frowned upon by environmental organizations. They rate special opprobrium if heated and air-conditioned.

Driveways however, are an entirely different story — if they are made of gravel. Gravel driveways have two important advantages over traditional asphalt drives: they are sustainable and cheaper. The savings can be considerable. Asphalt tends to cost roughly twice as much per square foot or perhaps a difference of a dollar or more, so a typical 50-foot by 12-foot driveway could save a homeowner hundreds of dollars.

Gravel is sustainable because it's nothing more than rocks and recycled material that essentially blends in with the earth. With a gravel drive, irregularly shaped stones the size of baseballs are laid down over packed dirt and covered with gravel. A good, inexpensive choice for the stone base is scalping from a stone quarry and for the gravel, recycled asphalt or, as it's known, RAP (recycled asphalt product). The porous combination allows for natural drainage.

It's possible community standards or pressure may prevent or make it difficult for homeowners to develop gravel driveways, so it's important to check with local building departments first. The only other concern is that it's not as easy removing snow from gravel as it is from asphalt. At the other end of the year though, it's easier to live with. Gravel won't burn bare feet in summer as easily as asphalt will.

Developers building more than one zero energy home could take a step to even greater home transportation sustainability by building common parking areas instead of driveways and providing their developments with neighborhood electric vehicles (NEVs), with their cost built into the price of all the homes. The NEVs are MINI Cooper-sized cars with top speeds of 25 miles per hour and limited ranges, which nevertheless can manage drives to railroad stations, shopping centers, schools and other local destinations. With the family car or cars out of sight and unused more often more homeowners may take to public transportation, biking or even walking, perhaps bare foot, which is about as sustainable as it gets.

FIREPLACES

No. Correction: Hell no! A hole in or beside the roof connected to the center of the house is unacceptable. No exceptions. Not the attractive iron stoves a proper distance away from walls lined with heat reflectors and opened only when there's a fire burning wood pellets in it. Nothing. The fireplace has been a loser on sustainable and efficiency grounds since the dawn of central heating and has no place in passive design.

3

Eyes On The Target

JAKE LUHN THOUGHT IT WAS TIME to start developing highly energy efficient homes when he became chief executive of LifeStyle Homes in 2006. It was "the right thing to do," he said. Still, he had to sell homes and make money doing it. However "right" it was, he needed to make sure that if he put in the time and money to build a house he could sell it profitably. He didn't want to make building any more complicated than it was. Whatever went into the house had to be available through traditional outlets at reasonable wholesale prices and he didn't want his crews working with any new products or materials that were beyond their abilities to use them.

Selling the houses meant giving customers proof, backed by numbers, that LifeStyle homes were better. The Melbourne, Florida, builder would build mid-priced production homes as he had before, but they would have significantly lower utility bills than those in homes the same size in the same area. Then LifeStyle's assertions that their homes were better would have more credibility. Quality would come at a price, but buyers would know exactly what they were getting in return.

The more he made his homes more energy efficient, the more he would cut their utility bills and the more his homes would stand out. There would be compromises in the name of cost-effectiveness, something of a step back for every two forward, but the endgame would be zero.

His new strategy was at the time an unusual one. Still, he wasn't alone in his thinking. Similar thoughts were percolating at other, mostly local and regional production builders, like Artistic Homes in Albuquerque, New Mexico, Carl Franklin Homes in Dallas, Ideal Homes in Norman, Oklahoma, Wathen-Castanos Hybrid Homes in Fresno, California, Tommy Williams Homes in Gainesville, Florida, G.W. Robinson Homes, also in Gainesville, Cobblestone Homes in Saginaw, Michigan, and Transformations Inc. in Townsend, Massachusetts.

Knowing something about any one of these builders is to get a start on finding out how a zero energy home can be developed, at least in their area. Seeing what several of them are like is to get a broader picture that will give home buyers an idea of who may be capable of delivering an averaged priced zero energy production home. It begins with finding a builder and it may be possible to do so almost anywhere in the country.

All of the above production builders can be found on the Department of Energy's Builders Challenge list. Its directory has 109 builders — production, luxury and custom — in 34 states who by the end of 2010 had built at least one home since joining the program that was at least 30 percent more energy efficient than the standard new US home. Other builders in the program, like Transformations, may have built homes to that level of efficient, or better, but before joining Builders Challenge. The average for the 4,900 homes built was actually 37 percent more energy efficiency. Those builders exceeding the average might have reached zero by installing enough solar panels to fit on one side of the roof with room to spare.

Another useful directory is the DOE's Energy Star Builders directory. It's a far more extensive listing, with builders in every state, but the bar is set lower. Builders only have to build homes that are 15 percent more energy efficient than the standard home.

Yet another Department of Energy resource for finding builders is the Building America's Research Projects directory. It's a listing of over 40,000 homes built in nearly every state. Here, it's the home — meant as a showcase for developing energy efficiency ideas — that gets the attention. The builders of these projects can be found by scrolling the entire list or by first finding homes by state and cities and then the builder. Details of what exactly went into the house may be listed on the project's web page. If

The Oklahoma home (front and back) that was one of the first marketable production homes designed to use zero energy.

so, it's a good way of seeing what a builder is experienced in doing and if they're listed in the Builders Challenge and Energy Star directories too, as some are, that may be a confidence-builder in selecting them for building a zero energy home.

Still, there's nothing to say even a builder of standard homes can't make the transition. After all, Lifestyle was just another company building minimally code-compliant homes when Luhn decided to take it in another direction.

The Opportunist

Luhn was in a good place and time to make the change. Incentives, initiatives and encouragement were all around him. While energy efficiency is either ignored or lagging in many states, Florida builders had to meet higher standards and buyers were more likely to be aware of them. The state's building codes meet higher energy efficiency standards than those in force in many other states and Florida also kept up with advances in the IECC codes better than many other states. Florida also provided financial incentives for solar power at the time — the better to promote the Sunshine State.

If they hadn't read about it in the news, Floridians only had to look around them. Solar installations were becoming more common in Florida than almost any other state. In 2008, it ranked sixteenth in grid-connected solar capacity before moving up to third in 2009. It's also easier and less expensive to build more energy efficient homes in Florida than most other states. The total cost of heating and cooling, a home's biggest energy expense, is lower thanks to its climate. LifeStyle has a particularly favorable climate to build in since Brevard County, where Melbourne is located, hugs the Atlantic coast midway up the state and is temperate much of the year. When it's not, in summertime, temperatures don't reach the extremes that must be endured further south and inland.

Another advantage was Lifestyle's proximity to the Florida Solar Energy Center. The state-sponsored environmental research organization was a half-hour drive away and was a unique source of expertise, its staff having studied and worked on developing zero energy homes since the nineties.

A Melbourne, Florida, home with solar panels (5.76 kilowatts) and a zero energy rating.

Not that it would be easy. There was a learning curve to master. Luhn would be pushing efficiency beyond where most builders would go, not just because of the extra work and time, but the extra cost.

Within his own company, everyone had to really believe this was the way to go. Sales had to consistently drive home the message that the extra cost was well worth it. They had to have the confidence that if people walked away because of costs they'd be back after comparing the competitions' homes to LifeStyle's. Also, the change in direction was made more difficult by its timing. When he started building his SunSmart homes early in 2008 Florida's home building market, to say nothing of the nation's economy, was on the verge of collapse.

Still, Luhn stuck to his plans throughout the disastrous times. He sold 50 SunSmart homes that averaged HERS ratings of 60. By comparison, a standard new home is 100 and an Energy Star home is 85. Sixty was, according to his calculations, the most cost-effective rating and level of energy efficiency that would allow him to take the next step. In August

2010, he completed LifeStyle's first zero energy-rated home. It was an expensive experiment for more zero energy-rated homes to come. The $417,000 home in a gated community was a large house for a zero energy home — a 2,390 square foot four-bedroom three-bath house — but it was a start and with a big, forgiving 8 kilowatt solar shingle installation as part of the roof an otherwise HERS 60-rated home earned a HERS minus 6 rating. Among the energy efficient features were an air source heat pump, Energy Star appliances and a solar hot water system with a solar-powered circulating pump.

While mistakes were made and work had to be redone, the home became the model for a 14-lot community of market-priced near zero and zero energy production homes. They'd be around 2,000 square feet each and cost in the low to mid-$200,000 range with 5.67 kilowatt roof-mounted photovoltaic panel installations standard.

The Pioneer

From its start in 1994, Carl Franklin Homes in Dallas built homes that used little energy and whatever they did use, they used efficiently. They were small (1,200 square feet to 1,400 square feet) and boxy three-bedroom, two-bath houses. This made them cheaper to build, heat and cool and easier to maintain for the lower income, affordable housing market it was serving.

The homes also encompassed the features that time and again would separate energy efficient homes from standard houses. Structural insulated panels were used to build the envelope, geothermal heat pumps provided heating and cooling, tankless water heaters produced the hot water and ductwork incorporated into the home's conditioned or lived-in space kept heating and cooling from being lost in the winter and summer, respectively.

Steve Brown, who co-founded the company, came by his ground-breaking work serendipitously. A structural insulated panels (SIP) maker approached Carl Franklin with a proposal that in exchange for discounted panels the builder would use only their SIP for the homes they were plan-ning to build. Carl Franklin accepted the SIP maker's proposal and Brown sought out other manufacturers of energy efficient features for comparable deals. He found them with a premium maker of geothermal heat pumps (GHP), tankless water heaters and energy recovery ventilators (mechanical ventilation is needed in SIP construction) and incorporated them into his homes as well.

His houses became a national laboratory. The US Department of Housing and Urban Development and the National Association of Home Builders used them to try out new technology. As the pumps, heaters and ventilators became standard features in Carl Franklin Homes, Brown was advancing a necessary step in mass marketing. He was providing an economy of scale for energy efficient features to bring down the price of highly energy efficient homes.

The energy efficiency gains were impressive. Early on, Carl Franklin Homes collected utility bills from buyers for over a year and a half. For a 1,240 square foot home, utility bills averaged $32 a month. By comparison, one homeowner showed them bills from his previous conventionally-built residence averaging over $70 per month.

Making money wasn't easy though. Brown needed to keep his profit margins narrower than the competition and trust in volume. He built 20 to 40 affordable homes a year selling at from $110,000 to $135,000 (in 2010) plus several custom-built houses, where he could get a better spread on margins, charging $450,000 on average. Eventually, he opened his own SIP factory to further cut costs and expand the business by selling SIP and putting up just the SIP shells in Texas and elsewhere, though mostly in the South.

He made some changes over the years. He switched to air source heat pumps (ASHP), concluding that geothermal heat pumps amounted to "overkill." The ASHP, while less efficient than GHP, were good enough to do the job for his small homes at a much lower price. He also changed from 2x4 to 2x6 board construction and to spacing the boards at 24 inches from 16 inches. Triple pane windows replaced double pane windows, improving insulation.

If he lagged anywhere it was taking the last, almost formal step. As solar panel prices fell dramatically in the wake of the Great Recession, he decided in 2010 that the time was right. In conjunction with the Oak Ridge National Laboratory — another Federal contact, this one with a long history of doing research on energy efficiency — Brown prepared to build his first zero energy production homes.

The "Builders Challenge" Stars

Wathen-Castanos's road to zero went from simple to complicated the closer they came to their goal.

The Fresno, California-based builder opened for business in 2005 building Energy Star rated homes with the aim of quickly moving down the energy efficiency scale. They hardly took a breath when in 2008 they joined the Builders Challenge during its first year. "We can do better," said their president, Mike Nimon, of the Builders Challenge standard. And they did.

Wathen-Castanos built 319 homes that qualified for the Builders Challenge by the end of 2010. Only three other builders surpassed them in the entire country, just one of which also built in a single area. But reaching HERS 70 was only a "marker" for the builders. They got down to HERS 60, and liking what they saw, thought they could go even lower. The climate was right in more ways than one.

Fresno is one of the hottest towns in the country. Ninety-seven degrees is the *average* summer high temperature. It's not unusual for homeowners to run up monthly air-conditioning bills of $600 in July and August and a builder who knew how to take an axe to that figure could attract home buyers.

Wathen-Castanos did just that, cutting air-conditioning bills nearly in half at HERS 60. They also found that the added cost wasn't as much as they might have expected. With greater insulation levels in the building envelope, including the windows, the company could replace a four-ton air conditioner with a two-ton unit.

Efficiency worked as a sales tool. Considering the country was by then in the midst of the Great Recession, they were pleased with their sales and aimed for higher energy efficiency, hoping to reach zero in two stages. They made progress by building low-income housing and chopping off another ten on the efficiency scale.

In 2010, they took one of their most efficient homes and for the first time added solar panels to the roof — a 4.6 kilowatt system. This got them closer to zero than any house they had previously built. It fell short because while the house was built to produce as much electricity as it consumed, it was not an all-electric house. Gas was used for heating, to provide hot water and as fuel for cooking. (The furnace and central air conditioning were highly efficient and a gas tankless water heater was installed.)

It was nevertheless a big step forward for Wathen-Castanos. They didn't have any idea how it would work out, so they built it to be a model home in a new development to be sold at a later date. The house cost more per square foot than their other homes. Where its approximate future sales price would be $280,000 for a 2,000 square foot home, Wathen-Castanos's other homes ranged in price from $128,000 to $270,000 for homes that were from 1,100 square feet to 2,300 square feet.

What they found out from their most ambitious and costly effort was that they were facing the "law of diminishing returns," said Nimon. "Buyers didn't want to spend any more to get more." Reducing air-conditioning costs by half appeared to be enough. Until demand catches up with the greater efficiency they are capable of producing, Wathen-Castanos reluctantly pulled back to the safer ground of HERS 60 where buyers think its homes are the coolest.

Dedicated Leader

Jerry Wade, the second-generation builder who owns Artistic Homes in Albuquerque, New Mexico, didn't always care about energy efficiency or renewable energy. He was too busy building homes — so much so that he became the biggest builder in the state, knocking out 800 homes a year. They were small homes built without frills for first-time buyers and selling for under $100,000.

That all changed in 1999. Wade and his three sons met with representatives of the Department of Energy's Building America program and what they had to say made sense to the Wades. They committed themselves to building energy efficient homes and transformed their business model. Within the next decade, they had switched from building homes heated and cooled by a combination of gas and electric to all-electric homes. They changed the framing to two-by-sixes from two-by-fours and replaced swamp coolers (a device that cools air by evaporating water and is common in Albuquerque's extremely dry climate) with central air conditioning.

The homes were tighter, better built, heavily insulated, more comfortable, far more energy efficient — and more expensive. They didn't price

An Albuquerque, New Mexico production home that with optional features added earned a zero energy rating.

themselves out of the middle class, but they weren't building starter homes any longer either. For most of the time market forces were at their back blowing gale winds and just about every house sold in the booming Southwest, but even the Great Recession didn't stop their prices from climbing. From 2008 to 2010, the cost of the average Artistic home went up from $182,000 to $216,000 to $232,000.

The company was different too. "We have sacrificed," says Tom Wade, the oldest son and the only one to see the transition through. Artistic dropped from number one to fifth in the state. In 2008, they built 175 homes and, with the Great Recession battering builders everywhere, they fell to 160 and then 100 in the two years that followed. Yet, they had no intention of turning back to the way things were in the last century. Wade thought they were doing relatively well compared to the competition and they were pushing forward. Their goal was to have every home they sold a zero energy home.

In 2008, they built and sold their first home that qualified for a zero energy rating, one of the first production homes in the country to make the grade. By the following year, they had sold 11 zero energy-rated homes, more than any other production builder in the country.

All were built to order; that is, buyers picked out one of Artistic's standard, though highly energy efficient homes, and added the zero energy option. Costs ran from $42,500 to $61,900 more than the same home without the package. Another 18 homes sold that used 65 percent less energy than standard homes. Artistic's new basic home was not far behind either. They averaged 49 percent more energy efficiency than the US standard.

With every home built exceeding the Builders Challenge qualifications, Artistic became among the program's leaders. Two hundred twenty of their homes made the mark as of the end of 2010 — good for fifth place. They were also leaders in building LEED-certified homes, making them the rarest of production home builders. Indeed, the company won the 2010 US Green Building Council's Outstanding Production Builder award for a $273,000 three-bedroom two–bath, 1,540 square foot zero energy-rated home that also won LEED's highest honors.

They weren't content to sit back and wait for buyers to discover them, either. They went after them. They expanded their operations to neighboring Colorado, one of the more eco-friendly states, and went to great lengths to find new markets, like pitching their homes at gun shows, where they would find enthusiastic buyers who had the same visceral loathing of paying money to utilities that they had for paying taxes to the government.

They had one pitch over the middle too. Artistic guaranteed all buyers the cost of their heating and cooling bills. If they went over the estimate, Artistic paid the difference. Better still, zero energy home buyers were guaranteed their entire utility bill. Wade says they've never yet had to pay out any money.

The Forerunner

R. Carter Scott saw the future of building early on and took one step after another straight into it. An award-winning restorer in Lexington, Massachusetts, he started Transformations, Inc. to build energy efficient homes there in 1993, two years before the Building America program got underway. Four years later he started installing his signature advance in energy efficiency — super-insulated double walls — into the homes he built. In 2005, he won the Energy Star Custom Builder of the Year Award from the New England Joint Management Committee and followed that up by breaking ground for his first single-family development the next year.

It was the 40-house development on Coppersmith Way described in Chapter One. One of the first homes was his own, an all-electric house with a geothermal heat pump. All the homes around him were speculative production houses selling at mid-range prices built in classic boxy New England styles that naturally lent themselves to passive design. In keeping with passive design principles, his houses were going to be smaller than the median-sized house and 60 percent more energy efficient than standard homes.

That was two years before the Department of Energy called on builders to develop homes that were 30 percent more efficient than standard as part of its new Builders Challenge program. Already beyond that, Scott was ready to answer a higher calling. He entered the Massachusetts Zero Energy Challenge, a 2008 statewide contest, with one of the houses he was

The second-place finisher in the Massachusetts Zero Energy Challenge.

building in Townsend. It would not only be developed to produce as much energy as it used, but also, as required by the contest, to be an affordable or market-rate house. Before Scott's entry was even finished, it was featured on the Discovery Channel. The house, which was affordable, costing $195,000, with a HERS minus 2.3 rating, came in second in the contest, but the 1,252 square foot house was a winner outside of it.

With the attention the Discovery Channel-featured house and Coppersmith Way were getting, several developers signed up Scott to construct communities in Massachusetts consisting only of zero energy-rated homes. By 2011, he was developing 33 of his houses in Easthampton and 8 in Devens. He was also working on a 24-unit condominium complex consisting of duplexes and triplexes, as well as single-family zero energy rated homes, in Harvard, Massachusetts.

Even these were walk-ups to higher standards yet. In 2011, he was planning on entering one of his Townsend homes in the NESEA contest to win $10,000 for a one-year zero energy home and was working on a project to develop a home with HERS rating of minus 38.

The Super Salesmen

To say that Tommy Williams Homes is the poster boy for zero energy home builders isn't quite right. To say that the Gainesville, Florida, builder of moderately priced homes is the poster boy for home builders across the US is closer to the truth.

The builder became worthy of being a poster boy in January 2010. That's when Tommy Williams Homes sold its first zero energy-rated home — two weeks after the $367,000 three-bedroom, two-and-a-half bathroom, 2,250 square foot house went on the market in the midst of the ongoing Florida real estate tsunami. It was also a prime example of hard work and planning paying off. Management worked on the project for six years, starting with little enthusiasm for even the idea of it, but working up to it.

Even Todd Louis, vice-president and marketing director of the firm, who was given the job of seeing it through by Tommy Williams, owner of the firm that bore his name, had his doubts. G. W. Robinson, another Gainesville builder, was working with the Building America program to build energy efficient homes and Louis's interest was strictly that of someone following a leader. Louis started working with the program in 2004 — three years after the other builder had signed up.

He thought the cost per square foot would be high compared to what it was for the code-compliant houses his firm was building. Still, he started

A standard zero energy-rated production home — front and back — in Gainesville, Florida.

to think the firm was in a good market for energy efficiency. Gainesville is a college town — home to the University of Florida — and it had the kind of educated population that might be willing to pay for energy efficiency.

The more he learned the more he liked thinking about ways to market it. One was to have prospective home buyers put their hands behind two windows, one more insulated than the other, while he shined a hot lamp on them so he could show shoppers how much cooler it was behind the more insulated window.

When the DOE started the Builders Challenge program, Louis quickly added Tommy Williams Homes to the list. By then, their homes were 40 percent more energy efficient than the standard home. In February 2009, the company took the leap and broke ground on its first zero energy-rated home. As soon as it was completed eleven months later, and debuted to local media coverage, a doctor and his wife bought the house.

By then, Tommy Williams Homes was already building a second zero energy home. This one was more in keeping with the firm's typical homes. It was a $260,000, 1,550 square foot house and it sold too, leading to a third home in the spring of 2011, a $270,000, 1,760 square foot house and of the three homes the one with the lowest price per square foot.

No one was more pleased with the way energy efficiency in general and zero energy specifically was working out than Tommy Williams. "Your granite countertops will never write a check for your electric bill," he said, alluding to the quote by Energy Secretary Chu criticizing Americans preference of granite countertops to energy efficiency, "but these new energy features might just pay for those granite countertops."

Or something else, since the zero energy-rated houses came with granite countertops.

4

Out of Sight Efficiency

A WORKER ARRIVES AT THE BUILDING SITE in a white space age suit armed with a spray gun attached to a noisy vacuum cleaner-sized machine. He or she — it's hard to tell — is given plenty of room inside. Anyone else working on the house clears out as the worker in white aims the nozzle at the wall and pulls the trigger.

The worker spreads a shiny, wet snow-like spray back and forth over the inside of the walls between the framing. As if alive, the spray becomes bubbly foam, expanding and spreading into every corner and crevice of the house's bare frame. The bubbles soon disappear, transformed into a lumpy, bumpy or prickly solid wall of white that covers wires and pipes and presses firmly against the lumber.

It's a satisfying job, because closed-cell, high density spray foam insulation actually lives up to what it appears to be doing. Spray foam forms an airtight barrier and provides structural support that makes it an excellent insulation to be used in developing a zero energy home. Yet as good a show as spray foam insulation puts on, it's not the only insulation that can make the grade, and it may not be right one for every zero energy home developer. It's not even the only spray foam. Another spray foam is open-cell low density insulation. Rigid foam boards, cellulose, structural insulated panels and insulating concrete forms are other options that all share similar properties with spray foams. Each also has its own set of advantages and disadvantages. In fact, any one of the four choices alone may not do the best

Closed-cell spray foam insulation being sprayed into the roof rafters (above) and open-cell spray foam being sprayed into the walls (below).

job in the walls, attic or foundation. Combining several types of insulation may provide the best protection against the heat and cold.

It's worth the effort of getting it right because having far better insulation than that found in standard homes is extremely important to developing a zero energy home. Heating and cooling is easily the biggest expense in a home's energy bill and ultimately the largest source of carbon emissions, not just from some distant power plant. Indeed, a majority of homes burn fossil fuels in the form of natural gas, oil and propane. In all, heating and cooling accounts for about 50 percent of the average home's utilities or over $1,000 annually. What kind of insulation a home has and how much can have a deep impact on how much that figure can be reduced. In fact, if there is one thing common to virtually every effort to build a zero energy home it's having superior insulation. Those efforts that succeed in reaching net zero very often have super insulation, a term given to the highest recommended levels.

Perhaps even more importantly, and unlike with passive design in general, super insulation is a job that can be and should be done at least on some level in all the tens of millions of existing homes. Super insulation can be added to many attics without disturbing family life below and a handy homeowner may be able to manage the job on their own at a cost they can afford.

Hiring professionals to do total super insulation retrofits including the ceilings, walls and basements can achieve even more impressive results. However, the cost will be substantially more than the cost for doing the same job in a new home. For homeowners still interested, or anyone working as their own general contractor, one source of help is the Insulation Contractors of America. They have a directory on their website with listings of insulators across the country.

Knowing What It Takes

Insulation can't stop heat from moving from one place to another. Insulation can only slow it down. Sooner or later, heat will escape in the winter and penetrate a home in the summer. By the same token, almost anything may provide at least some barrier or defense somewhere, even ice. Think igloos.

How well a material does in slowing down heat depends on how difficult a honeycomb-like obstacle course it sets up. The degree of difficulty is measured by its R-value, where "R" stands for thermal resistance. The higher its R-value the better job insulation does at slowing down the heat. A zero energy home developer will pack many more inches of insulation with higher R-values throughout the house, with a better fit inside the walls, than whatever is used in a standard new home.

However, there is a practical limit to how much should be stuffed into a zero energy house. Above a certain point the improvements in insulation are too small to justify the added costs and bulk in developing the home. The number rises with latitude, peaking at a cost-effective R-value for super insulation of 60. More heat transfer takes place vertically than anywhere else in the home with the sun beating down on the roof in the summer and heat rising from inside the home in the winter. The highest cost-effective bar is set at R-40 for the walls because less heat is transferred through them and more inches of insulation packed into walls would come at the cost of living space, something that shouldn't be a concern with the ceiling.

What's right for the floors or foundations is not simple though. Heat transfer down is less than through the walls, but some super insulated homes have more insulation under the slab than in the walls. Finances and climate are probably a better determinant than insulation level of what R-value is right for foundations. It may up in the 50s in the coldest climates and down to the single digits or none at all in the warmest where the ground temperature may be fairly close to room temperature all year long.

The Best Defenses
SPRAY FOAM
Done right, closed-cell, high density spray foam is just about the perfect wall insulation for developers, homebuyers and homeowners worried they'll need new or creative design solutions to get the insulation level they need in the wall. That may sound odd given the foam's magical properties and *Andromeda Strain* application, but the framing of the house can proceed as if it were a standard home.

Many well-constructed standard homes are framed with 2x6 dimensional lumber and it would be reasonable to do the same for a zero energy home using spray foam that has one of the highest R-values. Closed-cell high density polyurethane spray foam's R-value typically may range from 6 to 7 per inch. Multiplying the highest closed-cell spray foam R-value by 5.5 inches, which is the actual depth of the lumber, produces a total R-value in the mid-30s. It's a little short of the goal for four-season climates, but the foam is only the inner core of the wall. Since everything and anything will provide some insulation the total is a bit higher. It might even be possible to reach 40 when including the R-values of the interior walls, a house wrap and the siding. A builder would have to move to a wider framing material — 2-x-8s — to clear 40 with room to spare, which may not be worth the extra expense in wood, labor and insulation or the loss of living space, minor as that would be. The further south the house is the greater the temptation may be to fall back to 2x4s to cut costs for both the foam and framing and still reach zero with closed cell spray wall insulation.

Open-cell low density spray foam has an R-value under 4 and doesn't offer the protection against moisture that closed-cell does, but it may work in warmer, dryer climates. It looks and is applied the same as closed-cell, but with one difference. Closed-cell expands slowly so a good professional can fill the cavity precisely, while open-cell expands quickly and will overflow the framing. Excess foam is then shaved off smoothly with another power tool that looks like a cross between a saw and a giant comb. The end result is a smoother surface before any drywall closes it up for good.

In 2x6 walls, the lighter foam, siding and the like could yield an insulation value of R-25. Higher is always better, but not necessarily cost-effective, especially since open-cell tends to be cheaper on a per square inch basis (and what is shaved away doesn't hurt the pocketbook much).

Closed or open spray foam insulation is easier to work with in the attic than in the walls, even with the R-value bar set at 60. This assumes that the attic, as it should be with any zero energy home, is empty space that won't be used for anything. Spray foam may cover the floor to whatever depth it takes to reach R-60 or a total of about 8 to 9 inches thick of closed and 15 or 16 inches of open.

However, not everything about spray foam is desirable. Polyurethane is a fossil fuel-based compound and that's a drawback when trying to build a sustainable zero energy home. A number of brands replace much of the polyurethane with soy beans and, in some cases, recycled polyurethane. The combination may seem more sustainable and renewable, but it is really changing one set of problems for another. The soy is likely to come from genetically engineered plants grown on land better left for growing food since the world's population is increasing and arable land is decreasing steadily.

There are two things to say about this conundrum. No one has yet figured how to live entirely without using carbon, including zero energy home developers, and the foam can be recycled.

A particular drawback of closed-cell foam is that if there's a leak in the pipes or a need to replace some wiring, an electrician or plumber is going to have to hunt and hack their way through the foam to deal with the problem. Worse, it may take a while to discover a leak since, as noted before, closed-cell sets up a pretty good barrier against moisture so there could be a lot of water damage done inside the walls before anyone knows about it.

This could be true for leaking roofs too, although the moisture-repelling properties of closed-cell foam in the attic could be both a good and bad thing: good because everyone stays dry when it rains and bad because it'd be nice to know about the leak before there's extensive damage to the roof. Then again, if the barriers allow for any movement of the water around the foam the homeowner will know quickly enough.

Cost, though, may be the real deal breaker in developing new homes using spray foam, especially closed-cell foam. It will generally be among the most expensive insulations per square inch, costing thousands more to fill up walls and ceiling than if some other insulation material is used. One possible consolation is that with existing homes, homeowners and buyers can make significant inroads into the cost by doing the work themselves, at least for attic insulating projects where the skill demands are relatively low. Savings may run 30 to 50 percent over hiring professionals. (Labor costs are likely to vary more across the country than the price of the foam, thereby affecting the amount of savings.)

Everything homeowners need can be bought on the Internet, including a white, full-body outfit, spray kit and foam. The kit comes in a box that contains a spray gun, two hoses and two canisters containing chemicals that together produce the foam. The do-it-yourself version isn't exactly the same as the one the professionals use. Their equipment delivers the spray faster and that requires a more protective outfit. While the spray isn't toxic, breathing in blasts of it on a regular basis may cause respiratory problems. One-time do-it-yourself users may not even need a suit. Old clothes, including ski cap, swim goggles and a porous face mask can be used for protection from the spray. Using a kit, one pair of canisters delivers enough high density foam to cover 600 square feet one inch deep. For example, a 1,000-square-foot attic will require purchasing about 15 boxes to reach R-60.

For homeowners, buyers and contractors who would rather have someone else do the work, a directory of professionals can be found on the Spray Polyurethane Foam Alliance's website.

RIGID FOAM BOARDS

Rigid foam boards are the insulation choice for foundations in zero energy homes — or any homes. No other insulation can stand up to the conditions underground and still protect a home from heat transfer as well as the boards can for decades to come.

The boards are laid down under the slab and, in climates where the earth freezes during the winter, along the perimeter of the slab as well. The boards are typically four feet by eight feet by one or two inches. There are four kinds, listed in order of declining R-value: polyisocyanurate (polyiso or ISO), polyurethane (PUR or PU), extruded polystyrene (XPS) and expanded polystyrene (EPS).

All those syllables in words that will never come up in any conversation outside an insulation trade show do not bode well for learning the advantages and disadvantages of each and making an informed decision about which works best where and how. Even the people whose business it is might not know their names, much less what separates one from another. The bottom line is that when using rigid foam boards for the foundation the one that is easiest to find at the lowest price will be hard to resist. EPS has the lowest price per R-value and is, along with XPS, the most widely available.

Ironically, expanded polystyrene is, as was once said on old quiz shows, a common everyday object you see around the house. Egg cartons, coffee cups and packing peanuts are made from it. However, it gets confusing from there. People often ask for their coffee in a Styrofoam cup, but there is no such thing. Styrofoam is Dow Chemical's brand name for extruded polystyrene and is used for much sterner stuff, like insulation, so asking for either of them by name may not be the best way to order. For example, when asked over the phone what kind of boards his building supply company stocked one salesman could only manage, "like the coffee cup."

Color will do. EPS is white, while XPS is known as "Blue board" from Dow. "Pink" — as in "Pink Panther" — is from Owens Corning.

The remaining two rigid foam board choices will almost always be more expensive and may be difficult to find, maybe impossible for anyone wanting to get the recommended three quotes from the first three contractors or building supply outlets contacted. However, there may be exceptions. Rigid foam boards can be easily recycled whole. R-value will have suffered, but they'll still be a bargain at a price cheaper than new EPS. The catch is they literally come by the (tractor-trailer) truck load — as they do from Insulation Depot — which is more than enough for a zero energy home. They are also only available when the seller has them, not necessarily when the buyer wants them. Also, as will be frequently pointed out here, when making a decision to buy these panels it's good to take into account the carbon emissions from the truck carrying the boards from wherever they start from to the home.

Whatever boards are used, they're laid out in the middle of a five-part sandwich. The top is the slab followed down in order by a vapor barrier, the insulation, gravel and the earth, which has been dug out to accommodate everything.

EPS is R-3.7 so ten layers of one-inch-thick boards or five layers of two will provide the home with excellent or super insulation in many parts of the country. For example, a 32-foot-square saltbox house with approximately 1,500 square feet of living space would require 320 boards. Almost anything bigger or smaller in the zero energy size range will require cutting and pieces of some boards will wind up in landfills.

Adding perimeter insulation becomes a good idea the further north the home is located. One or two inches of board is placed against the outside of the slab vertically down several inches. Perpendicular to the vertical strip is a two-inch board extending out a distance of two feet or more. The perimeter insulation is buried beneath the earth.

Super insulation for foundations in cold climates can save hundreds, even thousands of dollars on concrete depending on material and labor costs and the size of the slab's footprint.

The savings are realized because the insulation means the slabs do not need a concrete footing. The footing would otherwise extend four feet down into the ground or below the frost line to keep the slab from shifting in the cold. However by installing super insulation a slab without footing is protected from the cold and also won't move — because it has no feet (joke).

Rigid EPS foam boards could also be used for the walls and the ceiling (i.e., the roof or attic), but getting super insulation out of it at a reasonable price may be more trouble than it's worth. Cutting up sheets and fitting them between the framing lumber in hopes of creating a tight fit would test the skills of an origami expert. That's why rigid foam board is nailed on outside the framing one full sheet after another with minimum cutting to fit.

However, this raises a space issue. If EPS is used, it will require 10 or 11 inches of insulation. Add a minimum of four inches in framing and the house would have a wall over a foot thick. Using rigid boards with higher R-values would result in a thinner wall, but higher costs.

Space is not a problem in the ceiling and 17 inches of EPS to achieve R-62 can be laid down with ease in a house designed for it. Rigid foam insulation can also be used in the ceilings and walls in existing homes, but the cost may be prohibitive in time and money. It's why existing houses don't make good zero energy candidates.

A big advantage of foam boards, though, is that older homes can profit greatly from just a little, as was the case in a 2009 New England retrofit. The drafty 3,200-square-foot 80-year old Arlington, Massachusetts, home guzzled a whopping 1,082 gallons of oil annually to heat the home. At the time it was costing the homeowners about $3,000, or more than three times the US average.

The homeowners could have saved money on their fuel bill with even a Christo wrap for insulation, but instead they had the walls and ceiling stripped and added two inches of foam boards to the former and three to the latter. It was enough so that the oil used in the furnace dropped to 350 gallons, a savings of two-thirds. The cost, though, was prohibitive at

$50,000 and might never have gotten done were the retrofit not so rare that the state's energy department helped defray some of the cost so the government could learn from the homeowner's experience.

Cellulose

Few things about developing a zero energy home can compare to cellulose insulation in combining energy efficiency and sustainability. Its content is about 85 percent recycled newsprint. The remaining 15 percent is non-toxic chemicals meant to reassure homebuyers and insurance companies that having cellulose for insulation will not lead to the house burning down or being devoured by termites. How much reassurance this provides may be limited since relatively few homes are insulated with cellulose, but it does meet fire codes.

Its energy efficiency is about as good as EPS, and it can be just as cheap if not cheaper to install. Cellulose is blown or sprayed in dry or damp, respectively, much like foam and fills up the entire cavity. However, it doesn't expand the way foam does to lend the framing structural support and, in fact, loses a bit of its R-value from settling. Cellulose is a little easier to apply, though. No uniforms are needed. Masks are a matter of choice and the equipment for blowing it into the walls or on the attic floor is available in major home supply outlets.

It all adds up to a terrific insulation choice for the ceiling. Eighteen inches worth will provide super insulation. Walls are another matter. Delivering super insulation may require construction techniques not found in every builder's play book. It will take 12 inches of cellulose to reach R-40. Does the builder use 12x2s or double walls? Could either become the new world standard for wall construction or would it be literally pushing the envelope too far? Are home buyers ready to sacrifice the living space such thick walls will mean?

If this raises too many questions, there is an alternative. Take the cellulose in the 2x6s and get a wall with R-20 value. It won't win many fans within a hour's drive of the US-Canada border, but it's not so bad that more cost-effective energy efficiency couldn't be picked up elsewhere. Way down south, however, filling a 2x6 wall with cellulose may work out just fine.

STRUCTURAL INSULATED PANELS

A given with structural insulated panels (SIPs) is that they form an incredibly strong, airtight link with each other and they require mechanical ventilation. This is true whatever the thickness of the panels or total R-value is. It's a big advantage for SIPs over framing since air leakages account for from 5 to 20 percent of heat loss or gain.

SIPs are factory-made panels that look like ice cream sandwiches with insulating foam sandwiched between two rectangular structural boards. The boards are manufactured mostly from composite materials made of wood, like oriented strand board (OSB), which is compressed wood chips. The foam slabs between them come in virtually the same varieties as in rigid boards, but for all practical purposes it's EPS that sells. Polyiso and polyurethane SIPs exist, but they're as hard to find as their board brothers.

Workers mounting a structural insulated panel into place.

SIPs are from 4.5 inches to 12.5 inches thick, but several sellers strongly recommend the 8.5 inch panels — right in the middle. If that becomes the choice, the SIPs will need a healthy boost on both the walls and in the ceiling to reach super insulation levels in cold climates. This could be achieved by attaching two-inch thick rigid foam boards to the wall SIPs and about eight inches of cellulose on top of the ceiling SIP. The 8.5-inch panels may be all that's needed where it's warmer.

SIPs are a tiny but growing part of the home building market. They're estimated to account for from one to two percent of the homes built and a home shell made of SIPs will likely cost less than a traditionally framed house. SIP builders can be found through their organizations, The Structural Insulation Panel Association, or Panelized Home Builders.

Fiberglass: Traditional Protection

Fiberglass is everywhere, and for good reason. It's been around the longest and was there when it was needed. That was in the seventies when utility bills jumped thanks to the oil crisis and increasing energy needs, like for air conditioning, which was in more than half of the country's home for the first time. It helped that fiberglass was seen as safe and the principal alternative, asbestos, wasn't.

Fiberglass was also cheap and easy to install. No wonder its batts, rolls and blown-in blankets went on to account for a steady 90 percent of the US residential market.

More of any insulation is almost always better than less, but if zero energy homes are going to make it into the mainstream the insulation market needs to be turned on its head. Fiberglass has the lowest R-value and if used in the walls would require many homeowners to accept far thicker walls and much less living space than they would even with cellulose, which would require considerable adjusting as it is. Also, while fiberglass is cheap, cellulose and EPS rigid foam boards are likely better values when used in walls. That's because, on top of its lower R-value, fiberglass doesn't fit or settle in as well as the other insulations and could very likely wind up costing more to reach super insulation levels in the walls. For example, an Oak Ridge National Laboratory study showed that a typical fiberglass wall installation lost 28 percent of its R-value.

Fiberglass could compete in the attic where, if a homeowner can make a bed, they can lay down fiberglass insulation. However, its potential is limited. It would take upwards of two feet to reach R-60 and that would be impossible to reach along the sides of many of the millions of homes that have gabled roofs.

Insulating Concrete Forms: An Alternative Defense

A SIP cousin, insulating concrete forms (ICF) are made-to-order pairs of white foam (mostly) polystyrene blocks several feet long. They're made into a unit with plastic or metal strips connecting the two blocks with space in between them and connected like Legos to other units to form a mold for the walls of the house. Concrete is then poured in between the foam blocks to create concrete walls with the foam insulation permanently in place.

They're a bit stronger than the already extremely strong SIPs and they protect against moisture as no wood product can, but they have a serious downside. They'll generally cost more than SIP and need much more energy to produce. The reason is that it takes about five times as much energy to make concrete than it does to manufacture wood products.

Their market share is more than twice that of structural insulated panel homes and contractors can be found at the Insulating Panel Form Association.

It's a Wrap

A question that might come to mind when viewing most new homes just before siding is added is: Who or what is Tyvek? Advertising for the next *Star Trek* movie? The name of the largest builder in America?

The answer is: neither. Tyvek is DuPont's home or building wrap — plastic sheeting sold in rolls. DuPont isn't the only manufacturer. It just seems that way because it commands 70 percent of the market. In fact, a search on the Internet finds at least 27 makers of house wrap, including DuPont competitors like Johns Manville (Gorilla), Dow Chemical (Weathermate) and Fiberweb (Typar). Having so many choices doesn't make much of a difference in terms of quality. A house wrap is basically a commodity: they're all pretty much the same.

What's nice about there being so many choices is that it helps make buying house wraps easy and that's a good thing because they're well worth buying. A house wrap is an inexpensive, but very good, hot and cold weather raincoat for homes. It protects the house from moisture — which can cause rot, mold and mildew — getting into the house, while also letting it out. It also provides another form of insulation by retarding air flow, a significant source of heat transfer.

The cost is another reason for having a house wrapped. It's small and should only have to be paid for once. The nine-foot plastic (polyolefin) rolls are from 100 to 200 feet long and prices range from about $0.80 to $1.20 a foot. A 2,000-square-foot rectangular home might cost about $250 plus labor to wrap.

There's no two ways about how it's done, either. The house is wrapped tightly and the strips from the roll are overlapped and taped together.

A plastic house wrap may not be for every home owner. A paper wrap is an alternative. It's even cheaper and would avoid having one more piece of plastic around a zero energy home, but it's generally less effective. However, it might be right for some houses. Paper wraps are more suitable for homes in wet climates with certain types of wood siding, such as redwood, cedar and manufactured hardboard siding.

The need for house wraps or any wraps is less in dry climates than in wet ones. Also, tightly constructed homes like modular homes made out of structural insulated panels won't benefit much from the airflow retarding feature in plastic and paper wraps if the homes are made right.

Except for these few exception, house wraps are as essential to super insulation as doting the i's and crossing the t's.

A Continuous Breath of Fresh Air

Good mechanical ventilation in most homes is provided when someone opens a window. This works well enough in spring and fall, except when sirens blare, cars spew exhaust and it rains. The system grinds to a halt in summer and winter, except for when the weather turns unusually mild, a meal is burnt or a pet behaves badly. When the windows are shut, the fresh air supply in many homes depends to no small degree on their sometimes miles of cracks.

Ventilation works differently in homes with super insulation (or any SIP construction, for that matter). These homes are so tightly sealed that they must be built with energy or heat recovery ventilating systems — ERVs and HRVs — to provide the home and its occupants with fresh air. A recovery ventilator moves the air through ducts that link the outside to every room in the house. While the window option remains, the system may run continuously throughout the year.

Air never blows in. Rather, it flows through the home at the same desired rate. The air is also cleaner and sweeter air because it is filtered and the intake vent is located in a side of the house where the air is cleanest (not facing the driveway or the street).

What separates a recovery ventilator from a fan with a filter is that, as the name suggests, it recovers heat. In the winter, the warm air leaving the house transfers heat to the incoming cold air, while in the summer the incoming hot air loses its heat to the cool outgoing air-conditioning.

The difference between a heat and an energy recovery ventilator is that the latter also removes moisture from the air. Which one a zero energy home developer installs depends strictly on the local weather. If humid, then it's an ERV, if not, it's HRV. The north, deserts and mountains are mostly HRV country, while the south is ERV territory. It's better to be in the former than the latter when it comes to shopping for recovery ventilators because ERVs are more expensive and more difficult to maintain.

An energy recovery ventilator: Outside and inside views.

A local HVAC (heating, ventilating, air conditioning) contractor experienced in installing these systems is the best source of advice on which one a home needs. They can be found at the North American Technician Excellence website's contractor locator.

In deciding which ventilator to buy three numbers stand out: price, energy usage and the sensible recovery efficiency (SRE). The last can be found at the Home Ventilating Institute's website. It lists about 200 ventilators with a jumble of numbers and graphs, but the SRE can be found there without much trouble.

SRE gives an idea about what percentage of the heat will be transferred. Anything in the 60 percent to 80 percent is good. As for price and energy usage, it might help to think about refrigerators when shopping for ventilators. They're both heat transfer machines and a ventilator may be on just as much as a refrigerator. (It will save some energy without any ill effects if it's shut down and some windows are cracked to get a breeze through the house in the spring or fall or when no one will be around for an extended period of time.) Their prices and energy usage are not dissimilar either. Efficient ventilators may cost about the same, while using more energy, as efficient refrigerators do. A good range for the ventilator's energy usage is from about 500 kilowatt hours to 700 kilowatt hours annually.

A ventilator with an efficiency rating at the high end and energy use at the low end will cost a lot more than if those numbers are reversed. Brand names from the HVAC industry like American Standard, Carrier and Trane mix with relative unknowns like UltimateAir. The last — not surprising, from its name — has about the best combination of low energy use and high efficiency of any ERV system, plus a price (possibly $2,000) that could cause sticker shock — more than twice that of competitors with pretty good efficiency numbers.

Balancing efficiency with cost is always a challenge in developing a zero energy home. This comes into sharp relief in buying a ventilator when the other half of the project is considered. If the recovery ventilator has its own duct work, this will add considerably to the cost of the system.

If the home has central heating or air conditioning, it may be possible to use those duct systems and there will only be the hook-up costs. If not, as is quite possible with zero energy homes, then a duct system will have to be built for the ventilator at a cost that will likely exceed that of the average ventilator price.

The ducts must be built within the conditioned, or living, space so as not to lose energy. That is, the insulation has to be between the outside of the house and the ducts. Whether that adds to the cost or not, is something to discuss with the contractor. It's also important to make sure that the system has been designed to have the shortest duct work as possible to save on costs.

In the end, a recovery ventilator system is an odd combination of choice and no choice. The work has to be done, and in just the right way, but there's no shortage of options in picking the right equipment.

The case for recovery ventilators keeps getting stronger too. The standard 21st century house is more in need of good ventilation than its 20th century counterpart because of tighter construction with a higher level of insulation. It's only going to get tighter, too, and even the buyers of standard homes may be ready to pay extra for a breath of fresh air come January or July when the windows are shut, the blinds are down and the drapes are closed.

5

Taking A Good Look

GLASS AND OPENINGS IN WALLS traveled on two separate tracks for many centuries before getting together. Absent a covering they could see through, builders thought small.

The Anasazi cliff dwellers pioneered passive design more than a thousand years ago with small, square open portals in their homes, favoring southern exposure, during their heyday in the dry, sunny American southwest.

Europe was no different in limiting open space in their walls. Chateau Gaillard, home to Richard the Lionhearted, King of England, Crusader and friend to Robin Hood, had relatively small, narrow openings in its walls — all the better to keep out the rain and enemy arrows, while keeping an eye out for the approach of same.

Glass had its uses, from beads to all sorts of glassware. It was just that no one could figure out how a flat, transparent version of it could be secured in window spaces. Not until the 1800's did the modern window — clear glass panes in window frames — become common. Yet, as insulation, windows were still holes in the wall. It hardly mattered though. The walls offered no better insulation and heating fuel was cheap.

When the energy crisis first hit in 1973, the need for insulation became apparent and it got stuffed into walls. Where there had been R-2, there was now R-10. It was a big improvement.

Not even that much could be said for windows. Then and now a pane of glass does little to slow down the comings and goings of heat. Fifteen percent to 25 percent of a home's heat gain and loss occurs through the average set of windows. As a look at the product list of many window manufacturers will show, a simple single-pane window averages about R-1 today.

A window's R-value doesn't have to be that low. Since the late nineties it has become easier to buy windows that are virtual operating systems designed largely to take advantage of solar energy and provide levels of insulation unreachable, if not unimaginable, in the past. They don't come close to insulating as well as walls packed with super insulation, but they've come a long way. Research and development has led to a dramatic improvement in R-values or, as they say in fenestration circles, U-factors, which is the inverse of R-values. New windows available today have R-values rated as high as R-11 or U-0.09. Add insulating window treatments, including drapes and blinds or shades, and the total R-value compares favorably or sometimes exceeds the R-value of a standard new home's wall filled with fiberglass batts. It doesn't make for super insulation, but the holes have been plugged up.

Ironically, the glass in windows hasn't changed much. It's still a transparent solid, or liquid or whatever (science hasn't come to an agreement on what it is) made mostly of silica, silica sand, quartz silica or just plain sand, as it has been for nearly a millennium. It's what's been done to glass and how it's used and framed that makes it different now.

A good window is no longer just a single pane in a thin wood frame. Instead, as many as three specially treated panes or, possibly, panes and inner films with spaces between them containing air or an inert gas, are packaged together. Wood is just one of a number of the framing materials that can be used and there are more ways to open and close the windows than in the past — as well as to have them not open at all. Each choice will have an impact on how well the windows help insulate the home.

Those choices will show up in the price, as well as decide what the insulation values are. Highly efficient windows can be one of the single biggest expenses in developing a zero energy home. It may cost upwards of $10,000 (at $60 per square foot of window area) to fill a modest-sized house with windows that have high insulation properties.

The benefits are in greater comfort and lower utility bills. Depending on where the house is located and other factors, the savings could be more than 25 percent, according to the Efficient Window Collaborative.

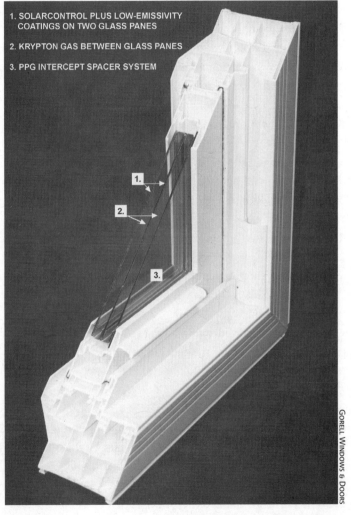

1. SOLARCONTROL PLUS LOW-EMISSIVITY COATINGS ON TWO GLASS PANES

2. KRYPTON GAS BETWEEN GLASS PANES

3. PPG INTERCEPT SPACER SYSTEM

1.
2.
3.

GORELL WINDOWS & DOORS

A cutaway of a triple-pane gas-filled vinyl-framed low-e double-hung window.

Not that only the best windows will do. Home buyers can spend less for less efficient windows and still reach zero energy by spending the savings on efficiencies in other parts of the house. In fact, depending on such factors as climate, labor costs, the kind of windows bought and a home's orientation, a window can cost less and be less efficient and still produce lower utility bills than more expensive and more efficient windows.

The fallback position that always works is to do what the Anasazis would be likely to do if they were around today and have as few and as small good glass windows as possible.

Installing windows is, like attic insulation, an energy efficiency job that can readily be done in existing homes, as well as in houses under construction, though it's better left to professional installers. Replacement windows will, however, cost more in labor and materials than original windows will. Installing replacement windows requires more work since the old windows have to be removed; not so with originals. Replacement windows will also cost more because installing highly efficient original windows in a home under construction will be merely an upgrade over the efficient windows any contractor would install today, while with replacements the buyer is starting from scratch.

However, for older homes extremely efficient replacement windows may be well worth the extra money. They will almost certainly be far more efficient than what they are replacing, whereas the same window installed as an upgrade is not likely to make as great a difference. The old house will be rendered much quieter too, while a new house window upgrade will make a smaller difference in sound levels. Finally, the difference in utility bill savings will be greater for the existing home than the new one.

More Than Meets the Eye

Choosing new windows, super efficient or not, can make living in a cave sound appealing. There are six common window operating mechanisms, five framing materials and three gases to consider on top of the hundreds of manufacturers and countless possible sizes, shapes and prices.

Selecting windows need not be completely exhausting however. Windows in a mainstream zero energy home that don't hit two key targets can be quickly eliminated. They need to have good insulation properties;

R-values should be at least R-3 and possibly exceeding R-5 in the colder climates. And they should cost, on average, under $50 a square foot (hopefully, below $25 a square foot) in 2010 dollars.

It would also be very helpful if whoever is responsible for selecting the windows has had good experiences with their manufacturer and in having them installed. Shipping, quality control and sealing become much more challenging jobs where high performance windows are concerned because they are heavier and more complex than traditional windows. Greater care also needs to be exercised to seal these windows with their thicker frames.

Still, there's more to know. All the other factors that go into deciding which window will work best in a zero energy home are not mere window dressing. Reaching zero depends on sweating the details.

Fortunately, windows come with labels that have the U-factor and as many as four other performance ratings that put into numbers how energy efficient a window is. The other four are:

- **The solar heat gain coefficient (SHGC)** is a number between 0 and 1. The closer it is to one, the more solar heat it lets in and the closer to zero the less it allows in. High is good in cold climates; low in hot ones.
- **The visible transmittance (VT)** is another number between 0 and 1. It's a measure of how much light gets through a window. High is good in cold climates; low in hot ones. It and the SHGC generally come as a pair.
- **Air leakage (AL)** has the same range too and the lower the number the less the air leakage. Low is better anywhere.
- **The Condensation resistance (CR) number** — between one and a hundred — tells how well the window resists condensation, which produces cold spots. The higher the number the better, though not much of a concern in warm climates and the least likely to show up on labels.
- In the interest of sanity, knowing if these four numbers are high, low or middling should be enough. With R-values (U-factors), it doesn't hurt to be specific. In most parts of the country, lower than two (higher than 0.5) is undesirable. Three (0.33) is acceptable; four (0.25) or more is better — except in the Deep South where a little more flexibility might work well enough.

What Will Get the Best Numbers?
PANES

A double pane of glass is common and triple panes are becoming more common. A double is necessary to get a window to R-3, which qualifies for an Energy Star rating. Triple panes are needed to reach R-5 and above. As might be expected, the more panes the heavier a window becomes. However, there are some triple pane windows, like those made by Serious Materials, that have two sheets of clear film instead of glass placed between the two outer panes to help keep weight down. Amory Lovins, chairman of the Rocky Mountain Institute, has the Serious Materials windows in his Snowmass, Colorado, zero energy home, called Banana House for the bananas he grows there.

Three panes or two panes and two sheets will cost more than two panes, all other things being equal, and for most of the short existence of triple pane windows, they have been too expensive for most middleclass buyers. However, more manufacturers are entering the market and their prices are becoming more competitive. A determined shopper may be able to buy them and stay within budget.

Among the positive signs has been a Department of Energy program begun in 2010 to promote volume purchases of original and replacement R-5 windows, which are virtually all triple pane. Sellers who enlist in the High Performance Window Volume Purchase Program are expected to charge no more than $4 per square foot above that charged for Energy Star windows (R-3 or U-0.30 to U-0.35, except in the south where it's R-1.7 or U-0.60).

There's a catch, though. Buyers must order a minimum of 20 windows for new construction and 15 for replacement windows to get this deal. That's a lot of window space for a zero energy home. Even if every window were relatively small — say, 3 feet by 5 feet or 15 square feet — that would be 300 square feet or 20 percent of a 1,500-square-foot home's floor space.

Still, the listing is a place to find R-5 windows and there's no reason why the companies can't sell fewer windows if buyer and seller agree on a price. The program is worth looking into just for window shopping because it lists the most popular windows being purchased through the program.

GASES

Inject argon, krypton or a blend of the two to replace the air between panes of glass and the R-value will improve. Krypton, the heavier, rarer and more expensive of the two inert gases, will do more to increase the R-value than argon and, for now, there's no way to get to R-10 without it. Unfortunately, its high cost and appearance in few homes makes krypton alone an unrealistic choice for most zero energy developers — leaving the zero energy mass market to argon and, possibly, the blend, for the foreseeable future.

COATINGS

A metal oxide coating called low-e (for emissivity) is applied to the glass during manufacturing to control the light and radiant heat entering the house. Whatever coating is applied will affect the SHGC and VT of the glass. The best part of choosing a low-e coating is that they are climate-specific and just asking for a low-e coating should insure that the buyer gets the right coating for their house's location.

Buyers have no way of knowing whether they get it or not — anymore than they would with their choice of gas. However, it may give a buyer some peace of mind to ask what SHGC and VT they're getting and see if it corresponds to what they should get for a house in their location. Remember, you want high SHGC and low VT in cold climates and the reverse in hot ones. The Efficient Windows Collaborative has more specific examples of what's best in different climates.

OPERATING MECHANISMS

Windows can be opened up and down, left and right and in and out to allow air to enter and exit the house. They can be closed the same way to prevent air from getting in or out, but at this job they don't work as well. They just can't entirely stop the air — and whatever energy it has — from getting in or out. How much air penetrates or escapes depends significantly on the operating mechanism.

Double hung windows are two sashes with glass in them that are opened and closed by sliding the sashes up and down over two parallel tracks. They have more air leakage than any other type of window, but they've been the window of choice for over a century and will likely remain among the most common, widely available and cheapest for years to come.

Single hung windows are double hung windows that only open from the bottom. They too have above average air leakage.

Sliding windows work much the same as single hung windows except they slide left or right. They have above average air leakage too, and could cost more.

Casement windows open and close in and out from the side and have two significant advantages over the sliding and hung windows. They open up entirely and have below average air leakage when shut. However, they are much more expensive because they are operated with a crank and the mechanism adds about 50 percent or more to the cost of the window.

Awning windows operate the same as casement windows, except they are hinged from the top instead of the side. They cost top dollar and have low air leakage ratings like casement windows. In fact, they may be classified as casement, but they are better at keeping rain out when open.

Fixed windows don't open and are the tightest of all windows, making them an especially good match for zero energy homes since ventilators provide all the fresh air a home needs. They cost less than casement and awning windows too.

Taking into account total cost and air leakage rates, zero energy home windows could have a combination of fixed and hung windows with casement and awning breaking through into the lineup if the desire is there and there's room in the budget.

The National Fenestration Research Council provides a directory for finding manufacturers that produce the above types of windows, and many more. (Another directory at the same address can provide a ton of information about windows, but only by looking at what each manufacturer can and can't provide separately.)

SASH AND FRAMING MATERIALS

What a window sash and frame is made of helps determine its insulation value and air leakage rate.

Fiberglass: Insulated fiberglass helps improve a window's R-value and air leakage rating more than any other material. It's also durable and made from abundant natural resources that when made into window frames can be painted. It is however, expensive and hard to find, accounting for about one percent of the window market.

Wood: It looks great. It's natural, takes paint well and has insulation properties nearly as good as fiberglass, but wood is easily the most expensive framing material, especially if it is Forest Stewardship Council wood. It's also the most difficult to maintain.

Vinyl: It's the cheapest and that's why it's the most popular. It provides decent insulation too and is quite sturdy, but it can't be painted and, as noted previously, it contains hazardous substances.

Composite wood: It could be an alternative to wood or vinyl because it's a mix of vinyl and (recycled) wood. It's more durable than wood and less toxic than vinyl, but more costly than vinyl and not as attractive as wood.

Aluminum: It's the poorest insulator with no compensating strengths.

Realistically, vinyl is the most viable choice for zero energy homes today. In shopping for R-3 to R-5 and possibly higher there just isn't anything else widely available and almost nothing at a price worth it to middle-class buyers. Energy Star has a directory of window manufacturers. Fiberglass comes in last with 16 sellers. Vinyl is first with 275 — with aluminum at 30 and wood and composite at 53.

Window Treatments

Windows are like the story of *Dr. Jekyll and Mr. Hyde.* During the day they do good things, providing light, a view of the world and, for many homeowners, warmth. At night, all that is done with and, indeed, some of a window's principal values are turned against the homeowner. Instead of providing them with a view of the world, they allow the world to look at them. Privacy is lost so shutters are closed, shades or blinds are lowered and drapes are drawn — leaving the windows invisible for more than half the time.

Window treatments — as shades, drapes and the like are known collectively — serve as a defense against a window's shortcomings. Besides providing privacy they can help protect a home against unwanted heat transfer in the night and, sometimes, the day.

Their R-values run from about R-2 to R-8. At the high end are highly insulated honeycomb shades. Hunter Douglas is one of the few manufacturers of high performance shades, claiming an R-value range from R-6 to R-8. A three-foot by five-foot insulated honeycomb shade will cost hundreds of dollars — more than many of the windows they cover.

Simpler shades, Venetian blinds, wood shutters and floor-length drapes have R-values in the R-2 to R-3 range at a fraction of the cost to cover the same sized window, with the exception of the shutters. Their cost will be closer to that of the high-insulation shades than to the cheaper window treatments. All window treatments will provide significant help keeping the summer heat out of the house, though they won't do much to keep the heat in during the winter.

Combining blinds and blackout insulated drapes with an R-5 window would provide the R-value of an R-10 window alone, but would likely cost less. The combination would also protect the home from summer heat better than the super-performing window. This deal looks even better when multiplied by the number of windows in a house. In all, the savings in the cost of windows, window treatments and energy costs would be thousands of dollars over the lives of the windows and the coverings.

Opening the Door to Energy Savings

Windows are not the only openings, or fenestrations, in a house. An entry door or two will also provide a way in and out of a home, though mainly for humans and their stuff. Lots of air will accompany them, less when the door is shut.

It is, or should be, far easier to buy a door than windows. Doors are sold in only a few sizes, shapes and materials. R-values are the only energy efficiency ratings used and there's no reason to have more than two doors. Prices are uncomplicated too and installation, whether original or replacement, is a relatively straightforward job done at ground level. Nor do they have to be handled especially carefully. Budgeting a few hundred dollars for a door attached to the average home is generous enough.

Even the history of doors is simple. Throughout most of time doors were made of wood. In the middle of the twentieth century homeowners were given a choice between wood and steel. Fiberglass doors were introduced in the eighties.

It's hard to go terribly wrong shopping for doors when developing a zero energy home and it shouldn't take up a lot of time. Doors are only a small factor in determining energy use and there isn't a big difference between fiberglass and steel, its closest competitor.

Fiberglass edges out steel because it's more durable and will save money on repairs and replacements over the long run. It also won out over steel in a 2007 *Consumer Reports* article. Steel has the edge on price, however, so a good buy on a steel door is worth considering.

Both fiberglass and steel — with foam insulation cores — top wood because wood is far more expensive and less energy efficient than the other two. R-values for the thickest insulated steel and fiberglass doors are in the range of R-11 to R-12, while a solid wood door is just an R-3.

Shoppers need to keep a number of other points in mind, which are the same for maximizing the energy efficiency of almost any door.

1. Pre-hung doors are best. These are doors that come with frames. Not all homes have them. Pre-hung doors make for a better fit between door and frame and that means they're likely to have a more energy efficient seal.
2. Doors without glass windows are better than those with them. Windows cut down on energy efficiency and make the doors more expensive.
3. The foam core should be polyurethane instead of polystyrene. The former offers better insulation. The insulation of doors, like windows, is measured by their U-Factor; the lower the better. The National Fenestration Research Council gives the U-factor and other detailed information but it's very difficult to find unless you're looking for a particular door. Shoot for U-0.1 to U-0.2. Energy Star lists 34 fiberglass and 25 steel door manufacturers for its label, but gives no specifications.
4. Houses tend to have a front entry door and at least one other entry door to conform to fire codes. That should do it because even the most energy efficient door is less efficient than well-insulated walls.
5. Thick doors are more energy efficient than thin ones. Doors generally range in thickness from 1-1/8-inch to 1¾-inch and their R-value rises with their thickness.
6. Small doors are more energy efficient than big doors, but the difference is small among the standard sizes available. The typical surface

dimensions are three feet by eight feet and that should be fine for any zero energy home.

6

Cash Backs and Other Green Possibilities

A NY DEVELOPER WHO BUILT A ZERO ENERGY HOME in New Jersey by December 31, 2010 could have received $31,000 from the state's utilities. No one did, but in 2011 it was still possible to cash in on $26,000, along with other financial incentives offered in the state. Nor was New Jersey the only state where financial incentives were available. Rebates, grants, tax credits, zero-interest loans, low-interest loans and energy efficiency mortgages are among the financial incentives available across the country that can help bring down the cost of developing a zero energy home. It might even wind up costing less than to build a standard home.

Incentives are by no means limited to zero energy home developers, though. They are meant for anyone adding qualified energy efficient and renewable energy features or improvements to any building. It's just that a zero energy homeowner has more and larger incentives to apply for than do owners of other new and existing homes.

The US is awash with cash, tax breaks and loans for energy efficient and renewable energy features for home builders and buyers. Two financial carrots are available nationally. How many more a homeowner can qualify for and how valuable each of them is depends on the features and the location of the house. Cities, states and public utilities have financial incentives that extend as far as their borders or service areas and, depending on where the home is, its owner could receive incentives worth thousands of dollar.

They could also receive next to nothing. The simple truth is that the US is divided between the haves and have nots. The Northeast and the West is where most of the money can be found, although even in these regions the financial incentives are not what they once were. The Great Recession had a huge impact on the ability of states to fund financial incentives for energy efficient and renewable energy products and services. It might be years, if ever, before they get back to where they were in the earliest years of the century.

The shrinkage, elimination or absence of financial incentives doesn't mean zero energy homes won't get built. It may just mean that, lacking any national commitment, they're more likely to be developed in places with incentives rather than in those without them.

Financial signs of the times, top and bottom.

One area in which the impact of state and local incentives can be seen is with solar energy equipment, which would be found in most zero energy homes. Solar rebates are typically the largest financial incentives wherever they're available and may be worth in excess of $10,000. So far, the states that have had the most photovoltaic capacity (the maximum electricity output) have offered among the best financial incentives. California, New Jersey, New York, Connecticut and Massachusetts have had residential solar incentive programs that offered the largest rebates and, along with five other states offering solar incentives, accounted for 92 percent of the solar capacity in the United States, as of 2008.

It's not just homeowners that respond to financial incentives. Commercial, industrial, public and non-profit interests may not only tap into them as well, but might receive the most generous incentives in those states where they're offered.

Sunshine, high utility rates and progressive politics have also been factors in making solar power more appealing in some states than others. California is one example where other incentives work along with financial ones. Its government has enacted rules and regulations that encourage energy efficient and renewable energy development — so much so that the state earned the top spot in the American Council for an Energy-Efficient Economy (ACEEE) energy efficient state rankings from 2007 to 2010.

California's climate, location and utility rates also help to spur solar use. It's among the sunniest states in the country, so a solar panel on a roof in many parts of the state will produce more electricity than almost anywhere else. What it produces will be worth more too because electric utility rates are well above average in California and every watt produced will mean more money saved than in most other states. Add numerous state, local and utility financial incentives and an established pro-environment citizenry and it should be no surprise that California alone has three-fifths of the nation's solar capacity.

West Virginia, on the other hand, has almost no incentives, which helps account for its coming in 43rd in the ACEEE ranking. It's not sunny, it has the second lowest electric utility rates in the country and it depends heavily on coal not just to power its homes but its economy, all of which helps explain why it is far from the top ten in using solar energy. (It also has only two builders in the Builders Challenge program — neither of which had built a qualifying home during the program's first three years.)

Whatever the mix of motivations, though, financial incentives can make the biggest difference in making a zero energy home more affordable.

Summaries of the financial incentives offered by the states and Federal government are easy enough to find. The Database of State Incentives for Renewables and Efficiency (DSIRE) kept by North Carolina State University, under contract to the National Renewable Energy Laboratory, is an indispensable tool for learning about what government and private utility incentive programs are available. DSIRE's website is organized by types of incentives and the summaries come with links to government sites providing greater detail. In Canada a similar site run by Natural Resources Canada keeps track of national and provincial financial incentives.

DSIRE updates its site regularly, as it must. Incentives aren't necessarily built to last. One federal program offering tax credits on many energy efficiency products came and went in two years, from 2008 to 2010. The Great Recession forced some of the most generous states, like New York, New Jersey and Connecticut to cut back on their incentives, particularly when it came to solar. Several states no longer provide solar financial incentives and the total number of states offering them has decreased.

When states pull back, that may be worse than when the federal government reins in or ends its programs. States have led the way in distributing renewable energy and energy efficient financial incentives. How much of a setback the Great Recession will have on their efforts to encourage the building of more energy efficient homes equipped with solar installations may not be known for years to come, but it can't be good.

Since energy efficiency and renewable energy don't have enough of a presence in the US to fill a niche on its own, cutting back in the midst of a terrible market for home development and improvement would at the very least be more damaging than if it were done during more prosperous times.

It may be possible for private interests to leap in where there is a gap in necessary financial incentives. One such effort has been in leasing. Private solar leasing companies leveraged public financial incentives during the Great Recession to enable homeowners to install solar panel systems without having to buy them.

Whatever the incentive and however they're used there are a variety of them and they should at least be taken into account when budgeting for a zero energy home.

Federal

Tax Credits. These are the only major financial incentives available for homeowners from the federal government and they're good through 2016. Any homeowner who installs solar, wind or geothermal power equipment at their primary residence is eligible to receive a credit when they file their taxes for the year it was installed. The credit is good for 30 percent of the cost of the system, with no upper limit. As renewable energy systems are almost always five-figure investments, the credit will likely be worth thousands of dollars in tax savings. Any credit not used the year in which the equipment was bought may be carried over to the following year and so on until it's used up.

Energy Efficient Mortgages. EEMs are the only other federal financial incentive and it is small-bore by comparison. It allows home buyers and owners making energy efficient improvements to borrow more money than they would otherwise be able to, up to a maximum of $8,000. Homeowners must hire a HERS rater to advise them on choosing the energy efficiency measures. Dating back to 1980, EEMs have never caught on and account for only about one percent of mortgages.

State and Local Government and Utilities

Rebates. Anyone developing a home needs to hunt down rebates. They can cover energy efficient and renewable energy features such as heating and cooling systems, appliances and solar panel installations. The amount of cash back can run from a dollar for a light bulb into the tens of thousands of dollars for solar panel installations. The bigger the prize though, the harder they are to get. Few states, cities or utilities offer large solar rebates. For example, in 2011 California and 16 other states offered solar rebates ranging from $2.50 per watt down to $0.50 per watt. All the states, except Arkansas, are located in the Northeast or the West.

Getting the money will require some paperwork or online work. Buyers may be required to have energy audits performed on their homes and have the equipment installed by certified installers, which is a good idea anyway. They may also receive payments only in installments, such as when they make their purchase, when it's delivered and when it goes into operation.

Rebates for energy efficiency improvements will be likely easier to get. More states make them available. They're not as large as the rebates for renewable energy systems, but neither are the improvements as costly to pay for in the first place. West Virginia's only rebates, for example, are for appliances and the most money any West Virginian will receive for one appliance is $100 for a refrigerator. Maine has four energy efficiency rebate programs, as well as one renewable energy one, that can earn a homeowner anywhere from up to $3,000 for a major project like home insulation down to one dollar for a compact fluorescent light bulb (CFL).

Grants. Residential renewable energy and energy efficient grants are far rarer than rebates. Low-income families are likely to have the best shot at receiving what few grants are available, such as those awarded in New York and Montana.

Loans. Zero- and low-interest loans for energy efficiency and renewable energy features are scattered across the country. They may be available from the states, cities and utilities. The lower the rates, though, the harder they are to find. Still, even the highest rates were considered fairly low until the Great Recession hit. With 15-year mortgage rates below 4 percent in 2010 many of the loans are not the great deals they once were. In fact, some of the energy efficiency and renewable energy loans charged higher interest rates than banks did for ordinary mortgages.

However, as of this writing there are some good ones out there and it's worth checking DSIRE for them. Keep in mind, though, that these financial incentives can disappear quite suddenly. Iowa has zero-interest loans lasting 20 years to cover up to 50 percent of the cost for a variety of renewable energy projects, including solar electric and thermal and wind. Santee Cooper, a South Carolina utility, has zero-interest loans to finance solar installations, while Ashland, Oregon, and Fort Collins, Colorado, offer zero-interest loans for homeowners and builders that make energy efficient improvements. Vermont has had one of the biggest and best deals. It arranges loans for a minimum of $50,000 at two percent interest to finance solar installations — on top of rebates of $1.00 per watt.

Income tax credits. A homeowner needs to live in a state which requires its residents to pay income taxes for any financial incentives to be available in the form of tax credits. That leaves out Alaska, Florida, Nevada, New Hampshire, South Dakota, Tennessee, Texas, Washington and Wyoming. They don't have income taxes. Of that group, only Washington manages to provide for enough other financial incentives to rank among the leaders.

One of the more popular personal tax credits is for solar power equipment, which is in addition to the federal tax credit. The credit is generally limited to some percentage of the installation cost and a maximum dollar value. About 20 states offer this credit. New Mexico offers generous tax credits for homes with geothermal heat pumps and that earn high LEED certification scores.

Property tax incentives. Energy efficient and renewable energy features add to the value of a home and can be counted on to increase property taxes, which are levied locally and are fairly universal. However, the state can pass legislation exempting them in part or entirely from being included in calculating property taxes either over a period of years or for the life of the improvement. Again, solar installations tend to get the most breaks. How much depends on the locale, but with the median property tax equal to about one percent of a home's value, a $30,000 solar installation could save a homeowner around $300 annually. More than 30 states offer some form of property tax incentives.

Sales tax incentives. The sales tax scenario is similar to the one for property taxes. The range for state sales taxes in the US is from four to seven percent so, for example, sales tax exemptions on a $30,000 solar installation could save a buyer $1,200 to $2,800. More savings may also be available where there are local sales tax exemptions, as in New York City. However five states — Montana, New Hampshire, Oregon, Delaware and Alaska — can't offer a sales tax exemption because they don't have sales taxes.

Net Metering. The practice of net metering is in one sense the most important incentive of all. Without net metering, the spirit of mainstreaming zero energy homes would be broken. (DSIRE keeps tabs on it under its rules and regulations sections, not incentives.)

Net metering is the process by which homeowners and other building owners feed the excess electricity produced by their renewable energy systems into the local utility's electric grid and get credit for it. The amount they are credited by their electric utility is deducted from the electricity they use from the grid and their final bill is the *net* meter reading.

The difference is visible. For example, on sunny days when homeowners are out, their solar-electric powered houses produce much more than they consume, and the disk in their meter spins backward. At night the reverse is true. Electricity flows through the electric grid to the building and the meter spins forward. In a zero energy home the disk spends an equal amount of time spinning forward and backward over the course of the year.

Net metering's importance can be seen from the fact that the federal government has pushed it since 1978. Legislation was passed that year to prod the states into developing net metering rules and regulations. They moved slowly, at the rate of one a year, until 2005. New legislation that year helped push the pace up to a rate of four a year. By 2010 net metering had become perhaps the most widely accepted renewable energy policy in the country as 46 states had put into place at least some form of net metering. Only Alabama, Mississippi, South Dakota and Tennessee are still without it.

The utilities in most states that have net metering credit homeowners feeding electricity into the electric grid at the same rate they charge all their residential customers. Using the US average electric rate of $0.11 per kilowatt hour, homeowners could be credited over $100 annually for every kilowatt of solar panels in their installation. (Photovoltaic systems produce electricity during the day and since in most homes little more than the refrigerator is utilizing the power, most of electricity produced is fed into the grid and credited by the utility to the customer's account.) In two states, Minnesota and Wisconsin, homeowners may turn their systems into a revenue producer, albeit a small one. Local utilities must settle up with customers each month and should they produce more than they use the utility has to send them a check for the excess.

Still, net metering remains a work in progress that won't be completed even if and when the last four states come aboard. About a dozen states give credit only at the wholesale rate or "avoided cost," as it's called. In some states hooking up to the grid, or interconnection, can be time consuming and costly, requiring homeowners to pay fees and take out insurance.

The Interstate Renewable Energy Council puts out an annual scorecard rating states' net metering and interconnection — "Freeing the Grid" — that gives an idea of which states have hospitable operating environments for solar arrays. The scores are standard letter grades from A to F. Seven states led the class of 2010. California, Colorado, Maryland, New Jersey, Pennsylvania and Oregon received As for net metering and Bs for interconnection, while Virginia earned an A in interconnection and a B for net metering. (No states received two As.) Just 16 other states received passing grades of D or better on net metering and interconnection. That's a total of 23, or less than half the states, that met minimally accepted standards.

PACE Financing. The biggest objection to solar installations is their upfront cost, which has led some municipalities and private companies to come up with ways around that. PACE (Property-Assessed Clean Energy) financing is one way. Berkeley, California, started it in 2008. Berkeley gave up on PACE when financing the program proved too much for its resources, but not before other communities took notice. Soon local governments scattered across the country in more than a dozen states adapted the Berkeley model so the financing would work for their communities.

Using PACE financing, local governments grant loans to owners of existing homes to pay for photovoltaic systems. The loans are at lower rates than what they could get from banks and they are paid off through an increase in property taxes. The payments are over 20 years — 5 more than home equity lines of credit — so energy savings from the panels may be greater than the property tax increase. If the owner sells the house, the solar equipment, the debt and the property tax increase stays with the house.

Private Sector

Leasing. Some homeowners can lease photovoltaic systems instead of buying them. Of course, PACE is just a public variation of leasing and, ironically, private leasing got its start at about the same time. A number of companies, like SolarCity, SunRun, Solar Technologies and Sungevity, saw their opportunity in the passage in 2008 of the eight-year-long unlimited federal tax credit for renewable energy expenses. Homeowners with excellent credit can pay nothing down and any repairs or maintenance are free. They save money on their operating costs because their monthly bills for the lease plus their new electric bill is less than what they paid to the utility before signing the lease and having the panels installed.

They'll save even more if they choose a leasing plan that requires some upfront cash but will allow the leaser to make lower monthly payments. The solar arrays are owned by the companies, but homeowners may buy the panels after the lease ends in ten years or more, renew the lease or have the panels removed.

The first states these companies did business in were — no surprise here — in the West and the Northeast. California, Colorado and Arizona are the prime markets, but various companies also do business in Hawaii, Oregon, Pennsylvania, New Jersey, Massachusetts and Texas and national roll-outs would generally be the goal for all the businesses.

Leasing and power purchasing agreements (PPA), a similar way of getting solar power without buying it, still have a lot to prove, though. The number of customers solar leasing companies have is only in the thousands, which isn't enough for these companies to insure that the business will last as long as the leases.

Loans. For homeowners who want to own an installation, but don't have or want to spend the money for it, a loan might be the answer. The incentive, particularly for a homeowner with excellent credit in a low-interest-rate environment, is that by owning the panels they increase their home's property value, as well as potentially lowering its monthly operating expense, just as they would by leasing. It may work, too, for someone either taking out a line of credit for an existing home or adding the extra money to a 30-year mortgage for new construction.

Incentives may not be absolutely essential, but they work. If zero energy homes are going to be part of the housing mainstream by 2020, the chances of that happening are greater if the best incentives are available to all homeowners. Priming the pump, so to speak, will help increase the production of the goods and services that go into developing zero energy homes and bring down their costs so more will be bought — to the point where incentives will no longer be necessary.

7

All-Year All-Electric Comfort

Visit Belfast, Maine, in winter and global warming will seem very far away. The rural town midway up the state's long and jagged coast near a bay over 20 miles inland from the Atlantic Ocean appears frozen in time. Temperatures in the coldest state in the lower 48° average below freezing during the season with days below zero not uncommon. Frost covers forests of snow into spring.

Closed shutters and smoking chimneys are signs of the centuries-old battle against the cold. It's a dirty, costly battle too. A typical Maine home-owner will need an efficient boiler or furnace costing some $3,000 or more new and feed it about $2,000 worth of heating oil, the primary residential fuel in the state, every year. The cost of oil alone is about as much as the average American pays for all their utilities and more than three times what they'll spend — $662 annually — on heating, the biggest energy expense.

Matt O'Malia's two-story, 1,500-square-foot cube-shaped home in a field off Crocker Road is fighting the same battle as any of its Belfast neighbors. With its fire-engine-red clapboard siding the house appears to promise plenty of heat too and with just one window above the porch

GO LOGIC LLC

A Passive House in Belfast, Maine that produces most of the little energy it uses.

over the north-side entrance by the road, it projects a fortress-like defense against cold northern winds.

The expected warmth is inside the house, too, but not from the usual sources. There's no roaring fire sucking down cold air and sending carbon emissions into the atmosphere for there is no fireplace or potbelly stove. Nor is there a big sizzling, clacking, knocking or humming oil, gas or propane-fired boiler or furnace emitting its own fumes up a flue from the basement for there is no boiler or furnace — or basement, for that matter.

Instead, the warmth flows from a little electric heater that's easy to overlook. Close to the floor, the same color as the white wall it's attached to, is a standard baseboard heater two feet long that could be purchased in any big box home supply store or on the Internet for well less than $100. Three heat the entire first floor, which is mostly an open space that includes a kitchen, dining area and living room. There are identical baseboard heaters in the three bedrooms upstairs for a total cost of $270 plus an annual heating bill of about $200.

How so little can go so far is reminiscent of the joke about the heir who thought he had hit a triple in life, when he had been born on third base. The heater can warm the entire space not through any special power of its own, but because of the way the house was built.

Nowhere is that more true than in the wall on which the heater is mounted — or walls, because there are actually two. The outer one is made of 8.5-inch-thick structural insulated panels while the inner wall is 2-inch by 4-inch framing filled with expanded polystyrene (EPS). This way, the heater can spread its heat throughout the room and keep it warm because the walls, ceiling and floor do a spectacular job of keeping inside all the heat it produces.

Other facets of passive design help too. The modest space (by current standards), puts smaller burdens on the heater to fill the space and the insulation to block the heat's escape routes. In all, the house needs around a tenth as much heat as would be required to warm an average home — a job well within the heater's strength. In fact, a standard boiler or furnace put in its place wouldn't work as efficiently as it should.

A boiler works best when it works steadily. However, in a super-insulated house it will work in fits, revving up and blasting heat into the room that has nowhere to go before the boiler shuts down again, thereby overheating the house — all at a price many times that of the baseboard heater.

The house is light on the solar production end with just 2.8 kilowatts of power mounted on the south-facing roof, so there still will be a utility bill, but in terms of passive design, insulation and heating and cooling, it's all that can be asked for of a zero energy home.

Cool Choices

A baseboard heater and the right passive design can take care of winter in a zero energy home, but what about summer? What works best economically? One answer may be nothing, or nothing more than a zero energy home would already have, which is a heat or energy recovery ventilator. If that isn't feasible or desirable there's also room and central air conditioners to partner up with baseboard heaters.

Energy or heat recovery ventilators as a substitute for air conditioning would seem to be unthinkable. Air conditioning is one of the technologies that defines what makes living today better than any previous time. Since its introduction after World War II, the use of air conditioning has grown to where it's in 86 percent of homes and its portion of the utility bill is third to space and water heating at a cost of $394 annually for the average home.

Nor can the remaining 14 percent be considered holdouts. Some homeowners can't afford it and others, like many in Maine, where only eight percent of the homes have air-conditioning, don't need it.

Still, as tough a sell as it would be, the upfront and monthly savings from doing with just a ventilator in a zero energy home is worth considering in northern climates where air conditioning is common. By circulating the night air into the house a ventilator can provide a zero energy home all the cooling it needs in many places where air conditioning is considered standard. Since even in mid-summer the temperature in many areas will rarely exceed the high seventies, the recommended setting for air-conditioners, once darkness has settled around the house it can be naturally comfortable at night and through much of the day since super insulation will keep the cool night air in longer.

* * * *

Room air conditioners may be as tough a sell as no air conditioning. For every home with room air conditioning, three have central air and the ratio has been climbing in favor of central air for decades. It might be an even tougher sell for zero energy home developers. Their homes are supposed to be air tight and even a single unit in a master bedroom would punch a big hole in the house.

Taking it out of the high R-value triple pane windows each fall and installing it again each spring calls for serious behavior modification. It also calls for having double or single hung windows, which would not necessarily be present, and precious extra space where there is none (like a garage or basement). Multiply the number of room air conditioners — and seasonal labor — so as not to deprive children of what their parents have, even if it means overcooling their smaller rooms, and the chances of mainstreaming zero energy homes with room air-conditioners would appear to be a non-starter.

Central air, though, is not a major concession. It would be essential in the South and Southwest and not much of an economic strain there or anywhere if it was in a zero energy house. The fraternal twin 2,425-square-foot Rick Strawbridge homes in central Florida give an idea of why. The home that nearly reached zero energy when it was built had just a two-ton central air conditioner (half the size used in its fraternal twin across the road) with a 14.4 seasonal energy efficiency rating (SEER) . A two-ton system is small and not just by the standards of hot climates like Florida. It's small by any standards. Some manufacturers don't make anything smaller in their residential lines.

The efficiency rating, while exceptional when the house was built in 1998, wasn't a decade later. The federal requirement was moved up to 13 by then and 14 is the minimum needed to qualify for an Energy Star rating. If a Strawbridge home, which has more square footage than the US median home, can be kept cool with so small an air-conditioning system, it would seem zero energy homes may be able to do with the smallest central air systems available in most of the country.

That would be a one or 1.5 ton system and the cost could be less than $1,000 with a SEER meeting federal requirements or the minimum Energy Star rating. Goodman is a brand with a 1.5 ton system that often comes up at that price. It may cost three or more times as much for a three ton system, which is a minimal size for many conventional homes and with an 18 SEER, which is toward the higher end of the mass market range.

Duct work might not cost anything extra. Central air can possibly share the recovery ventilator's ducts. Determining what works in heating, ventilating and air-conditioning or HVAC takes some figuring out to get the right size system in the right places. It's calculated using two indispensable reference works. Manual J, which is a text used for calculating the correct heating and cooling load and Manual D, which does the same with determining duct sizes. Both offer guides on what input (insulation levels, climate, etc.) to use in the calculations and how to crunch the numbers. It should go without saying that they are available in electronic formats, but "manual" seems safe — for now. Manuals J and D are both published by the Air Conditioning Contractors of America (ACCA) and are available at Amazon.com.

A thermostat — a classic square or round manual or mechanical model — may be all a baseboard heater in a zero energy home needs. They can cost anywhere from $10 to $50, a price that will help keep a zero energy home on budget. After all, there may be one in every room. They're dependable and there are many choices from well known brands like Honeywell to lesser known names like Lux. They may also work with central air. Digital programmable thermostats lit by LED (with no mercury) are a reasonable alternative. They'll cost a little more upfront and over their lifetime because their screen needs electricity to stay lit, but can earn their keep through energy savings for homeowners who would rather set it and forget it.

"Smart" thermostats, though, may be carrying intelligence too far. They have exciting features like being able to program a thermostat from a computer outside the home, but the cost for the unit and installation charges may run into the hundreds of dollars. Mastering the systems may require too big an adjustment for homeowners, or they may set them so they wind up wasting more energy than they save. Of perhaps more concern is a subset of the population that has privacy and health concerns about smart thermostats. They worry over how signals may cause cancer and if anyone may be hacking into their home life. However, there's no reason not to look forward to the day when utilities install smart meters, with smart thermostat capabilities, that everyone will accept. That way the utility pays for the meter and the customer gets the benefits, which include not only being able to set temperatures, but control lighting use. Customers would also know how much energy they're using when, and how much it costs any time of the day.

Complete Package

Building a heating and cooling system starting with baseboard heaters is not the only all-electric solution. Heat pumps offer a far more efficient choice — more than any other heating or cooling equipment — at a price.

Electric heat is inefficient by itself because of how it's produced. Only 30 percent of the energy from the coal burned at the power plant reaches the home as electricity and is then converted into heat. Electric heat in a zero energy home does much better because it's using a clean and free energy source — the sun — as its electric source. Still, a zero energy home's baseboard heater falls short of the performance of oil, natural gas and propane boilers and furnaces. They turn 80 to 95 percent or more of the fossil fuels into heat because their source of energy is turned into heat directly at the home.

Natural gas leads the fossil fuel group in efficiency because little energy is used in transporting the fuel. Coal travels by train to power plants and oil and propane travel by truck to homes, while natural gas travels from its source through the pipes of the Interstate Natural Gas Pipeline, using much less energy in transport and losing little through friction and leakage.

Heat pumps are the most efficient heating and cooling equipment because they leverage the electric power they use. The electricity is not turned into heat directly, but into mechanical energy first. The mechanical energy is used to squeeze heat out of two unlimited and free sources, the air and the earth. What's more heat pumps do things that baseboard heaters, boilers and furnaces can't do. They supply air conditioning by simply reversing the heating process. The heat is removed from inside the house and replaced with air at a lower temperature.

The inside of a home heated and cooled by a heat pump has a different feel than a house with a furnace and air conditioner. It's comfortable and temperate as opposed to cycling between warm and cool. The heating or cooling is on almost constantly, with no peaks or valleys.

There are two types of heat pumps, air and ground, and they've both been gaining in popularity. In 1999, heat pumps accounted for 22 percent of the heating equipment in new single-family homes, while traditional boilers and furnaces had a 72 percent market share (baseboard and others made up the remaining 6 percent). Ten years later heat pumps were up to 37 percent, while conventional central heating was down to 56 percent; all but one percent of its loss was to heat pumps.

The two types of pumps have the same physics, but not price and efficiency. The ground or geothermal heat pump is much higher on both counts. While the air source pumps may be cost-effective in a zero energy home as an alternative to baseboard heating teamed with air-conditioning, geothermal systems tend to be too costly a choice except, possibly, under certain conditions.

They may work when the systems are sufficiently subsidized and that may very well be the case through 2016. Geothermal systems are entitled to the same 30 percent federal tax credit afforded solar and wind power systems. Air source heat pumps are not eligible for the credit. About a dozen states also offer rebates that help with some of the cost. Connecticut was the most generous by far in 2010. Through the state government and Connecticut's utilities it was possible up to May of that year to receive rebates of over $10,000. Demand was so great that the rebates had to be cut if the program were to continue, but homeowners could still receive as much as $6,500 — still several thousand dollars above what any other states offered.

If it's installed in an individual or custom-built home the system is more likely to be cost-effective at, to be inclusive here, the high end of the zero energy price range. That is, larger, more expensive zero energy homes could justify the higher costs of geothermal systems.

AIR SOURCE HEAT PUMPS

Air source heat pump systems (ASHPs) do the work of air conditioning and heating with components located inside and outside the house, just as with central air conditioning. In winter, a fan in the outside unit, which is indistinguishable from an outside A/C unit, sucks air into the unit so a condenser or compressor and coils containing refrigerant can extract the heat from it. The heat energy is absorbed by the refrigerant which flows into the house where a blower is housed for distributing the heat.

How the heat is distributed leads to a fork in the road leading to two types of ASHP: conventional and ductless or mini-split systems. Instead of sending the heated air (or, in summer, the cool air) through ducts to every room in the house, the ductless system deploys strategically placed wall units that heat or cool zones, which may be a room or rooms.

The single biggest disadvantage with an ASHP — and a serious one it is — is its performance at the extremes. On the coldest and hottest days they work much less efficiently and it may be possible that under those conditions residents will not be able to stay comfortable in their home. The drop in efficiency is worse in cold climates than in hot ones. Older ASHP shut down in the teens. Homeowners might want to consider a space heater or a baseboard heater for a back-up. The cold weather downside makes ASHPs more popular in warmer climates than cold ones.

The cost of installing duct systems for heat pumps will be comparable to what a homeowner would spend on ducts to heat and cool their home with a furnace and central air systems. It should be less for a ductless system in a zero energy home, however, because the ductless ASHP is more flexible than a duct system.

The duct system has one indoor unit that distributes the same amount of heat throughout the house, while a ductless ASHP may have four units, each with its own heat capacity. A zero energy home may do well enough with just two units, each of a different size. In a two-story house there would typically be one on each level, as in the case of the zero energy rated home in Townsend, Massachusetts. It cost $5,200 for a 12,000 BTU unit downstairs and 9,000 BTU upstairs.

The downside to a ductless system may be their aesthetics. The zone units stand out. They are heftier than baseboard heaters and, mounted up on the wall instead of down on the floor, they are easier to see.

ASHP manufacturers appear to see the potential concern. Mitsubishi makes one of the best ductless ASHPs, but in naming their system they didn't choose a word or phrase emphasizing its superior performance. They chose a name to draw attention to its trimmer profile: Mr. Slim. In a central heating and cooling world, though, where out-of-sight is part of the appeal, whatever is in a name may not be enough for some homeowners.

Ground Source or Geothermal Heat Pumps

A geothermal heat pump is a vast improvement over the ASHP — and anything else used to heat and cool a home — for one simple reason. It uses the heat of the earth, where the temperature below several feet deep stays between about 45 degrees and 55 degrees. Geothermal power is also in some ways a better renewable energy source than solar and wind. It's out of sight and more dependable than either — two more advantages over ASHPs as well. In fact, it should be able to maintain the same temperature 24/7/365.

In winter, the water circulating through tubing underground is piped up from under the house into the geothermal pump over coils containing refrigerant, which absorbs its heat. The refrigerant is then raised to a steady 95 degrees under pressure by a compressor. In the summer, the method is reversed. The home is cooled by circulating hot air out of the house — a process that is similar to the operation of a refrigerator, an appliance that the pump resembles. Maintenance consists of cleaning a filter every few months; the pipes are guaranteed to last 50 years. A fan and compressor contain all the moving parts in the pump.

Although the notion of tapping the earth's heat has been around forever and the basic technology has existed for decades, the many advantages have only recently begun to win widespread attention. The big reasons are concern for the environment and, more to the point, money. Although they are the most expensive heating and cooling systems, geothermal heat

A geothermal heat pump and a drawing of a typical horizontal loop that would be connected to the pump.

WATERFURNACE INTERNATIONAL, INC.

WATERFURNACE INTERNATIONAL, INC.

pumps are becoming increasingly competitive, even for homes in which an old furnace and air-conditioning system must first be removed.

The number of geothermal heat pumps shipped — industrial and commercial, as well as residential — more than tripled in the US from 2000 to 2009. A number of celebrity homeowners who use them have helped raised the technology's profile — like the country music star Toby Keith, the Home Depot co-founder Arthur Blank, the actor Ed Begley Jr. and former President George W. Bush. But the biggest driver is the cost of fossil fuel. After averaging between $5 and $10 per thousand cubic feet from 1985 to 2000, the price of natural gas went on a much bumpier ride to higher ground. At the end of 2010, it was over $15 per 1,000 cubic feet.

The payback period for geothermal heat pumps depends on a variety of factors, including the type of system, the installer and the location and size of the house. Typically, it takes three to ten years before fuel savings equal the cost of the pipes and placing them in the ground; indoors, the cost of traditional heating and cooling systems and geothermal installations may be the same. Of course, the greater the heating and cooling needs and the higher the fuel costs, the quicker the payback. A 2,000-square-foot all-electric home in New York City that is less than 10 years old needs 30,000 BTU/hour of cooling and 47,000 BTU/hour of heating and will save over $600 annually by switching to a geothermal heat pump, according to a calculator on the website of WaterFurnace, a geothermal heat pump manufacturer. A very different scenario emerges in Los Angeles. The same house would need 34,000 BTU/hour for cooling and 21,000 BTU/hour for heating and would save around $300 annually — doubling the payback recovery time.

While the savings are a function of utility rates as well as climates, they will almost always be greater in colder climates than warmer ones. The geothermal heat pump industry consistently puts the increase in efficiency of their pumps at 50 to 70 percent more than standard heating equipment, but just 20 to 40 percent better for cooling.

Not surprisingly, then, geothermal gets more interest in colder climates. Illinois, Pennsylvania, Ohio, New York, Minnesota and Indiana, which has the added incentive of being home to WaterFurnace, are the biggest markets for geothermal heat pumps. California, the overwhelming leader in solar usage, but not a cold climate state, is a middling market for geothermal heat pumps.

Just as those colder states order more geothermal heat pumps, there are also more certified installers in them. Often the states where the most pumps are sold are the ones where the most installers are located. The standard for installers is certification by the International Ground Source Heat Pump Association (IGSHPA) and eight cold states — Colorado, Illinois, Massachusetts, Michigan, Minnesota, New York, Pennsylvania and Wisconsin — have the most IGSHPA certified installers, with more than 200 each. .

Installers generally stick to one brand of pump to get better pricing from the manufacturer, so the installer and pump tend to be a package deal. The most desirable pumps carry an Energy Star efficiency rating. Among the brands earning that rating are WaterFurnace, ClimateMaster, Trane, Hydro Delta, McQuay and Econar.

A 1.5 ton to 2.5 ton Energy Star-rated system could cover a zero energy home, which is half of what most other homes would need. Prices for Energy Star equipment will run upwards of $3,000. "WaterFurnace is the Cadillac," said Steve Brown, head of Carl Franklin Homes. "But there are a lot of good pumps, and it's more important who puts in the system. You have to shop around to get the best deal."

Installers generally recommend three types of systems: those with horizontal, open vertical or closed vertical loops. A horizontal loop system, typically an E-formation that requires about half an acre, is recommended when homeowners have the space. It is generally the least expensive, and its costs fall further if it is part of new construction, because its installation can be combined with the laying of the foundation.

The cost of a loop varies greatly, from about $1,000 for a horizontal loop connected to a modest house in the West, where land is more available and often easier to dig up, to $50,000 or more for a vertical closed loop attached to a mansion atop New England bedrock.

A vertical loop, generally two or more connected branches extending more than 200 feet into the ground, is used the most often. It costs more because of the drilling expense, but few homeowners have the space for a horizontal loop.

There are also open vertical systems, which are drilled in much the same way as a water well and may be used when there is access to an aquifer. These may do double duty in rural areas by providing homes with drinking water.

For a relatively few lucky homeowners, there is an option that delivers the best of both green worlds. It's the pond loop, for homes near a body of water that is at least eight feet deep year round. There are no digging or drilling costs, just the cost of a Slinky-like tubing coil and the labor of placing it at the bottom of the pond or lake.

"It's generally the cheapest," said Kirk Bellanca, a co-owner of Enviro-Tech, an installer in Staatsburg, New York. "You should get permission from the town, but they're almost always very supportive. The fish like it, too. It becomes part of their habitat."

In a sense, two comfortable homes for the price of one.

CHAPTER 8

Getting Into Hot Water

MORNINGS START WITH THE COSTLIEST ENERGY RUSH. Showers, which use the most hot water of any activity in the house, are turned on and 20 gallons goes down the drain with each one. Shaving with a razor consumes another two gallons.

As the day goes on more hot water is used. Thirty gallons may be used in the clothes washer. The dishwasher will use another ten gallons (even more is used if the dishes are done by hand). Hot water will be tapped to prepare food (five gallons daily) and wash hands and faces (four gallons daily).

Day in and day out the cycle is repeated. By the end of the year, the clothes washer will have washed 400 loads, the dishwasher 215, and with all these daily uses a bill comes due — financial and ecological — for all the hot water used. The individual homeowner's out-of-pocket share amounts to about $300 or around 13 percent of the $2,200 annual utility bill.

This is the second highest energy cost in dollars and percent after heating and cooling. Clothes washers, the fourth biggest user of hot water after showers, baths and faucets, were in 84 percent and dishwashers, fifth, were in 66 percent of homes as of 2009.

Hot water is flowing through more showers and faucets, too. In 1998, the median new US house added on a half-bathroom. It increased to two and half from two, largely because more new homes were being built with three or more bathrooms and, with household sizes shrinking more people are able to take showers for as long as they like.

Reducing the amount of energy used to provide all the hot water a household needs, or more likely wants, requires greater energy *and* water efficiency. The former is achieved mostly on the supply side, or what heats up the water, and the latter is won on the demand side, or where and how the water is used.

Just how much zero home energy developers can or need to reduce it involves another juggling act of efficiency, utility rates and purchase costs. Chances are, though, that energy cost and use can be reduced by 50 percent or more.

Nor will savings only be limited to energy. Water efficiency will also lead to a smaller water bill for most households. The volume of hot water accounts for about $90 or a third of the median $278 water bill, according to the American Water Works Association. (The bill includes the cost of watering the lawn, washing cars and any other outdoor use, as well as the water consumed indoors.)

Necessity born of scarcity might be even a greater motivator. Droughts and shortage are a growing concern that may lead homeowners to cut back on the amount of water they use. In a poll by the Government Accountability Office reported in 2003, some 36 of 47 states participating in its water survey expected shortages within 10 years.

Developing a zero energy home that uses much less energy to meet hot water demand requires a change from the traditional storage tank hot water heater big enough to handle the morning rush. Storage tanks are virtually the only way water is heated in homes, accounting for 97 percent of the household market. That leaves precious little shelf space for competing products. Still, the alternatives in this small corner are common enough, with a fair share of name brand selections that handily beat the efficiency of a standard storage tank. They can be bought and shipped to wherever they're needed and should not be a challenge to plumbers, electricians and carpenters.

The main replacement — virtually all of that remaining three percent — is a relatively small resistance heater. No, it's not a baseboard heater. Although it is another metal coil housed in a protective metal casing, it's not much different either. The main difference is that instead of spreading its heat out and up through air, the coil heats water flowing through a pipe it surrounds. The unit is called a tankless or demand hot water heater.

Other options exist, but don't replace the tank. They're supplements to it or use a different technology to heat and store water more efficiently in a tank. They include a desuperheater, a heat pump hot water heater and a solar hot water heater. They are well-established technologies that can be bought easily enough and will deliver incredible efficiency, but they

Point-of-use tankless or demand water heater.

BOSCH

have their drawbacks. They represent another cost and create a level of complexity that may not endear themselves to homeowners. Indeed, since taken together they hardly amount to a market the size of a rounding error despite being around for many years, there's nothing to suggest the mainstream will be any more receptive to them in the future than it has been in the past.

Demand Side Economy

Fixtures and appliances that use less hot water without making washing any less satisfying or effective represent the demand side of cutting down on the amount of energy used to heat water. The less there is to heat, the less energy is used. Lower the amount enough and it almost doesn't matter what does the heating. That's why the more water use is reduced, the more appealing tankless systems become, much the same way a small, super-insulated space can be heated by a low-powered baseboard heater. In fact, unless a home's water use is below average a tankless system could be an expensive gamble.

To bring down the demand, homes need to be equipped with low-flow showerheads and faucets, plumbing layouts as short as possible and, where cost-effective, highly efficient dishwashers and front loading clothes washers. All of these will work for existing as well as new construction, with the exception of, if necessary, the short layouts.

SHOWERHEADS

In April 2010 the Environmental Protection Agency (EPA) added low-flow showerheads to its five-year-old WaterSense program, which is to water efficiency what Energy Star is to energy efficiency. To qualify for the listing, showerheads needed flows of no more than 2.0 gallons per minute (gpm) or 20 percent less than the 2.5 gpm standard. The action was taken after testing showed that showerheads could be more efficient without sacrificing the "feel" of the water. Showerheads that succeeded on both counts earned the WaterSense label.

The efficiency push was the first of any kind since 1992 when Federal guidelines mandated the 2.5 gpm standard at a time when flow rates were typically 4.0 to 7.0 gpm. Encouraging the use of slightly more efficient low-flow showerheads is not as big a move as the original guidelines, but it shows there's still the potential for significant gains in energy and water efficiency.

The WaterSense list is growing and by the end of 2010 included over 200 showerheads from 13 manufacturers, including American Standard, Delta, Kohler, Moen and Toto. More are beating the required 2.0 gpm flow rate and have reached as low as 1.5 gpm. It may be just a matter of time before showerheads have even lower rates. In fact, some manufacturers already produce showerheads with rates as low as 1.0 gpm and there are even 0.5 gpm sprays. That they are not listed with WaterSense doesn't necessarily mean they are better or worse than those that are. They may have simply not been tested yet.

Splitting the difference between high and low, a 1.5 gpm WaterSense qualifier could be the most cost-effective showerhead for a zero energy home. They need not cost any more than a standard showerhead, which can be bought for $10 to $50, and could cost less. The 1.5 gpm models will save 40 percent over the standard showerheads — more where they replace more powerful heads — on both the energy and water bills and the savings can be enough to recoup the cost of the showerhead in a matter of months.

For example, a WaterSense-qualified 1.5 gpm model would save an average of $6.58 monthly in water and energy costs over the 2.5 gpm models, according to Flex Your Power, California's energy efficiency marketing campaign. The savings would pay back the expense of an Alston 658, to name one 1.5 gpm model listed on WaterSense and selling on the Internet for $32, in just five months.

While they may pass the "feel" test with the EPA, the switch to 1.5 gpm or even 2.0 gpm might call for some behavior adjustment. A *Seinfeld* episode from 1996 played the 1992 law for laughs, showing Kramer buying a "black market" showerhead so powerful it knocked him off his feet. It wasn't so funny years later when a 2005 Lawrence Berkeley National Laboratory paper reported that 24 percent of residences were not in keeping with the Federal low-flow mandate. Asking consumers to adjust to another 20 to 40 percent reduction may take some convincing.

Still, getting down to 1.5 gpm represents the kind of easy energy and water efficiency gains that need to be part of a zero energy home. If the change is made, a generation from now will be just as content washing with a 1.5 gpm spray as their grandparents' generation was with 4 or more.

Where does this leave baths? They use 30 to 50 gallons of hot water and there's no way to reduce that number. That's how much water bathtubs hold and the only way to use less is to switch to showers or use a fraction of their capacity.

FAUCETS

Where showerheads go, so too do faucets. Their flow rate can be lowered even more easily just by replacing the nozzle, at a cost of a few dollars. Flow rates between 0.5 and 1.5 gpm are common. Bathroom rates tend to be towards the lower end, while kitchen rates are at the higher end. WaterSense only lists bathroom fixtures, more than 2,000 of them, but not their flow rates.

CLOTHES WASHERS

Shopping for a clothes washer can lead a buyer into a swamp of information. When choosing a washer on the basis of price and energy and water efficiency, shoppers should consider two options.

The first type of washer is a standard-sized Energy Star-labeled top loading model. The second is the front loading version. Models of each can be found with relative ease and they can achieve energy and water savings of 50 percent or more while keeping a zero energy home budget on target.

Energy Star clothes washers must be at least 30 percent more efficient than units that haven't earned the label. Many models do much better. While a standard model may use over 400 kilowatt-hours of electricity and 12,000 gallons of water annually, a huge selection of Energy Star washers use under both 200 kilowatt-hours and 7,000 gallons annually.

The cheapest Energy Star washers will get the gains nearly as well as the most expensive ones, sometimes as well or better. Also, the cost spread will be lower between inexpensive Energy Star and standard models than for expensive ones. While the difference between median priced standard and Energy Star models is $400, it invariably will be less with cheaper models. The extra cost of Energy Star washers will be earned back within their typical lifetime of 11 years and even faster with cheaper models.

If there are any disadvantages to Energy Star models, other than a higher upfront price, it's a lack of familiarity. Energy Star is little known on its own in regards to washers. They've increased their market share to over a third, but make up little more than ten percent of the clothes washer market.

Some three dozen manufacturers, including virtually all the major producers, make Energy Star models. Seven of the dominant brands — Frigidaire, General Electric, Kenmore, LG Electronics, Maytag, Samsung and Whirlpool — also have the most models to offer on the Energy Star list.

The front loader is a better option than the top loader primarily because it is more energy and water efficient. Also, by shopping around, a buyer might get that higher efficiency without a commensurate increase in price. Front loaders are space savers, too, since they can be stacked with the dryer, something that can't be done with top loaders — not an inconsiderable advantage in a zero energy home where using space efficiently matters.

Front loaders are at a disadvantage to top loaders in some ways. They generally cost more and need some special care. It's recommended that special detergent be used and consumers need to keep front loader doors open occasionally to ward off mold and mildew. Top loaders have a two to one edge over front loaders in the US, but front loaders are relative newcomers to the market. They were introduced only in the nineties — about 50 years behind the top loading washers. Nevertheless, there's good reason to think they have a shot at taking over the US market. They already account for 90 percent of European residential washers.

The entire list for all Energy Star models — replete with annual water and energy use — as well as an energy savings calculator can be found on the right side of the Energy Star clothes washer web page.

Another website, begun in 2010, does the hard work of shopping for clothes washers and other household products. It ranks the most efficient products and what they cost from a number of web sources. The top ten washers were broken up into large (over three cubic feet) and small (under three cubic feet) and were all Energy Star front loaders.

The site is called TopTenUSA, a nonprofit organization, and if the list doesn't have the most efficient and cheapest washer for sale absolutely anywhere, it'll do in most cases. With a few clicks, a visitor to the site can buy the model they want and have it shipped to their home, pronto.

The current best values among the large washers were two washers in a virtual tie: a Frigidaire model, ranked fourth and an LG model, ranked seventh. While a bit less efficient than the leader, they were less than half the price. They also used a quarter as much electricity as a standard top loading non-Energy Star model costing only about 25 percent less.

Any choice, top or front, Energy Star or not, will be even more energy efficient if buyers "use cold water for the wash cycle instead of warm or hot (except for greasy stains), and only use cold for rinses." The quote comes from the American Council for an Energy-Efficient Economy (ACEEE), but it may as well have come from any one of several other sources, like the California Energy Commission and the Consumer Energy Center. Manufacturer factory settings tend to support cold water washing too. Most settings are for cold or about 80 degrees, and warm or 100 degrees, not hot or 120 degrees. (I've given four sources here because it seems that human nature tends to associate getting things clean with using warm water.)

DISHWASHERS

Dishwashers are the polar opposites of clothes washers. They use more energy despite using far less water. The incoming water must always be hot — 120 degrees Fahrenheit — which helps explain why they need the extra energy.

As little water as they use, dishwashers are becoming even more efficient at using it. A standard model used just 15 gallons in the eighties, while the typical unit 20 years later used only 9 gallons. The standard was 6.5 gallons in 2010 when Energy Star was 5.8 gallons, which was reduced to five gallons of water a cycle in 2011. As with clothes washers, a complete list of Energy Star qualified dishwashers can be found on an Energy Star web page.

Energy Star models are again the right ones for a zero energy home. A huge brand name selection is available, including the same ones manufacturing clothes washers plus several other producers like Asko, Blomberg, Bosch and Kitchen Aid.

Dishwashers listed by efficiency are at the TopTen site, which also cal-culates the savings for them. Ironically though, the savings listed show that for what they cost none of the top-rated dishwashers would earn back the price paid for them with their portion of utility bill savings.

A better strategy might be to hunt among the websites of the most familiar brand names. Frigidaire, for example, had several Energy Star models that cost little more than their standard units, but much less than their most efficient models. The verdict: the more inexpensive Energy Star dishwashers are better buys for a zero energy home than the more expensive models. The more expensive models cost too much to justify the expense and will almost never pay back the investment in them.

Supply Side Efficiency
Tankless Water Heaters

Demand or tankless water heaters are the antithesis of the standard hot water storage tank delivery system. The conventional system is always on, heating the water, whether it's needed or not, wasting energy and money. More energy and money is wasted as the water loses heat on its way to its destination. Storage tank water heaters also take up space that the more modest-sized zero energy homes can't afford to lose. Wrapped in insula-tion, they'll require a 16-square-foot closet of their own to store and pro-tect their unsightly bodies. In extreme cases, they give basements a reason to exist by being a place to stick hot water storage tanks — but then base-ments are mercifully a dying species.

As the names they are known by make clear, tankless or demand hot water heaters heat water only when needed, and don't take up any storage space. A tankless water heater typically occupying one or two cubic feet can be mounted out of the way on the wall. It's often small enough so that it can be placed out of sight under sinks, behind a faux medicine cabinet mirror, inside kitchen cabinets, set in bathroom shelves or recessed in an internal wall.

They can be installed in one central location or, because of their small size, at several or all water outlets. The advantages of placing the heater at what is called the point of use is that the unit can be matched to the water needs of that water outlet, be it a shower, sink or dishwasher. The hot water also arrives faster than if it's coming from a central source and will lose much less heat traveling inches instead of however many feet away it's located elsewhere in the house.

In the two-and-a-half-bathroom house there might be five units of varying sizes, including one in each bathroom, one in the kitchen and the fifth wherever the clothes washer is located. According to the Department of Energy's Energy Efficiency and Renewable Energy program, the greatest efficiency — as much as 50 percent over storage tanks — can be achieved if you install a demand water heater at each hot water outlet.

The advantages of having a central or whole house system are that there's only one purchase to make and one installation to pay for. Whether it's a central system, several units or one for each outlet, the arrangement that works best for a zero energy or any home will depend on the size of the household, the gallons of hot water used, the number of fixtures and appliances using hot water, utility rates, the cost of a unit or units, labor expenses, the desired water temperature, the ground water temperature and each heater's flow rate.

While most of these factors would just as well figure in the sizing of a storage tank, the last three are key for the tankless heaters.

Flow Rate. The capacity of a tankless unit is its flow rate, specifically how many gallons of hot water it can deliver in a minute. This is irrelevant for tank systems since the water is already hot and waiting to be used. A tank's capacity is simply the gallons of water in it and when it's all gone, it's gone for about an hour, while the tankless heater keeps that hot water flowing. Rates run from 0.5 gpm on up at 0.5 increments. Prices rise significantly with flow rates. In a zero energy home there should be no need to reach beyond four or pay more than a thousand dollars. As already seen, Energy Star clothes washers can fill up faster at 2 gpm, than older standards at 4 gpm. The same efficiencies apply to the other water outlets so that their flow rates may be lower than they have been in the past without affecting how they feel. Showers can flow at 1.5 gpm, dishwashers and the kitchen sink at 1 gpm and bathroom sinks at 0.5 gpm. A three-bedroom two-and-a-half-bathroom house would require 8.5 gpm if all the water outlets were turned on at once (a highly unlikely scenario).

The same tankless heater can deliver water at different temperatures at different rates; the higher the rate, the lower the temperature boost. It's not always clear from the product information, though, what rate the manufacturer is talking about and the buyer has to read the brochure to find out. It's safe to say that if two heaters are listed with the same rates but one costs more, the more expensive unit will deliver hotter water.

Groundwater temperature. In choosing a tankless water heater it is often recommended to assume that the intake water temperature is 50 degrees. Yet, that only applies to the colder regions of North America, where the groundwater may even be in the 40s. In much of the country it can be in the 60s and may even reach into the 70s in the Deep South. The difference counts when sizing a tankless water heater. A cheaper tankless heater used in a southern home will do the job of producing hot water as well as a more expensive model in the north, just the way someone driving a standard sedan could win the Indianapolis 500 if it were given a big enough head start.

Output temperature. The temperature needed varies from one water outlet to another. Only the dishwasher will need hot water — actually, the hottest at 120 degrees — at all times. Showers and sinks will need 110 degrees at best, while the clothes washer will do mostly without any hot water, except on for the occasional stain removal job at 120 degrees.

Realistically speaking a whole house unit could provide all the hot water needs for the average sized household or larger, keeping an occasional eye on water use. That's because of the lower demand from the outlets in a zero energy house as a couple of simple scenarios for maximum demand show:

1. Two hot showers, the kitchen sink and a bathroom sink running at the same time would require 4.5 gpm at 105 degrees.
2. Clothes washer washing stained clothes and dishwasher operating at the same time would require 3 gpm at 120 degrees.

A whole house electric tankless heater would be a good bet to do either job, and many less demanding ones, where the intake water is above 60 degrees. Less than 60 degrees might require some holding back. Stiebel Eltron and other manufacturers sell whole house models for around $1,000. By comparison a 50-gallon electric hot water storage tank would cost half as much, and it could handle the two most demanding jobs above anywhere in the country.

A point of use solution — again, with many possible configurations — can handle any demand, but at a higher cost. One way to cut down on the complexity of installing the best combination of point of use heaters could be to buy them from a single producer, like Rheem. They have six different point of use models, one of the largest selections on the market. Five units from its RTE series could provide all the hot water for a zero energy home with two and a half baths. They'd be mounted in the bathrooms, kitchen and wherever the clothes washer is located. The choice of models would depend on the flow rate and temperature rises needed, but could meet all the hot water needs at a cost of about a $1,000 in the South. In the North the need to substitute one or two more powerful units might drive the cost up several hundred dollars.

Shopping around some may lower the costs, north and south. Other makers of point of use electric tankless heaters include Eemax and Ariston, as well as Bosch and Stiebel Eltron. A 2006 Northwest Energy Alliance study indicates that labor could add anywhere from a few hundred to around a thousand dollars to the cost.

Rare, But Considerable Picks

Desuperheaters. Homes that have heat pumps or central air conditioning systems can add a desuperheater to their systems and get free hot water. Heat pump manufacturers sell them as separate units that go with their system. They work by capturing the heat dumped by the air conditioner or the heat pumps during the cooling seasons. The size of a football, they cost a few hundred dollars and will pay for themselves. The further south the house is the faster the return. Down south, they might even pay off the cost of the hot water storage tank too.

When attached to air conditioning, a desuperheater can supply a home with all of its hot water in the summer. A heat pump can do the same, but also provide at least some hot water much of the rest of the year too. Traditional storage tanks would be left to do whatever the pumps or air conditioners don't do. An added benefit with the geothermal system is to improve its air conditioning efficiency since the hot air doesn't have to be pushed back down into the ground, only as far as wherever the hot water storage tank is located in the house.

Air source hot water heat pump. An air heat pump water heater tank can be the perfect solution for a relatively small number of home owners. Not to be confused with the heat pump, it is a separate unit — part of another storage tank system that nevertheless labors under the same principle. It drives the ambient heat of the air — free energy — into the water. They work well and provide considerable utility savings, but only where it's never below 40°F. With consistent moderate air temperature they always have a source of relatively accessible heat to pump into the water stored in the tank. Home owners will also need a large separate space to store the heater, like a garage or an unused basement or attic. This is because the pump tends to throw off cool air, which is not something most people want in their house from fall to spring. Given these facts, these pumps have not been a big seller and look to have little potential for becoming one, especially in zero energy homes, which are not likely to have garages or basements, nor want a thermal break in their heavily insulated attic.

Solar thermal hot water heater. Solar heaters can have the greatest impact on the cost of making water hot. They'll save anywhere from 60 to 95 percent on the hot water end of utility bills. However, buying the system will come at a price of thousands of dollars, far higher than any of the other alternatives to having a stand-alone traditional storage tank.

Nor is that the end of the upfront costs. Solar heaters don't work all the time, like during stretches of cloudy weather, and they need a backup. It may be a storage tank or a tankless heater, adding more money to upfront hot water costs.

Solar hot water heaters have a couple of other unattractive qualities. They may take up roof space that could otherwise be filled by solar electric panels. They have a different look than the photovoltaic panels and may make more of a fashion statement than a homeowner may care to make. They also don't work their best in colder regions or in winter. Colder regions happen to be where the sun shines least — even less when the weather turns frigid. Of course, these happen to be the places and times when hot water is appreciated most.

It all comes back, however, to the fact that solar heaters are big budget expanders. Production home builders and buyers will tend to need some financial incentives, which do exist, to sign up, but the main satisfaction from owning a solar heater is eliminating nearly all the carbon emissions associated with heating hot water.

Getting Out of Hot Water, but Into Even More Energy Efficiency

Toilets have nothing to do with energy, at least not directly. They don't use electricity, but it takes electricity to pump water to homes. The cost will be born directly by the homeowner if they have their own well and indirectly if they get it from a water system. It will show up in their electric bill with the former and in their water bill with the latter. Reducing the amount of water toilets use will have the biggest impact on either cost because toilets use 28 percent of the daily household total — more than any other outlet in the home.

It's easy enough to make toilets more water efficient, too, thereby freeing up funds for making the home more energy efficient. New high-efficiency toilets use just 1.28 gallons a flush, or about 20 percent less than the 1.6-gallon standard set by Congress in 1992. WaterSense lists over 600 toilets that meet its 1.28 gallon standard. Many are dual-control models. They have two buttons — one delivering 0.8 gallons and meant to flush liquid; and the other delivering 1.6 gallons, for solids. They include brand names like Kohler, American Standard and Toto and may cost no more than even some of the cheapest standard toilets, with prices under $300. The operating savings are modest, perhaps $20 a year in water costs, but as there's no need of payback time it's money that goes straight back into the pocket.

9

Cool and Bright Ideas Well Done

T HEY ARE THE THREE ELECTRICITY USERS without which a house is not a home: refrigerators, lighting and cooking appliances are in virtually every occupied home, new or old. Although not as important and a much later entry into the house than the other three, clothes dryers are close to being as omnipresent (and yes, more dryers and stoves run on electricity than gas). They are in 80 percent of all US homes and have been increasing their household share since their postwar debut. Individually none of the four uses as much energy as the water heater, but as a group they use considerably more and at least the first three appliances present opportunities to reduce the amount of electricity needed to do their work. The choices made in buying each of these three major appliances are also opportunities to get a better deal on price that could free up hundreds of dollars in budget money for other efficiencies.

If this money flows into lighting it will give homeowners the chance to install in their house what may be remembered for generations to come as the one super energy efficient breakthrough technology to enter the marketing mainstream in the second decade of the century. This is light emitting diodes or LED lighting, as it is commonly known, and, as described later in the chapter, LED is literally entering the market as Edison's incandescent bulb, LED's 19th century predecessor, is leaving.

Refrigerators

Buying a good, inexpensive, energy efficient refrigerator is like throwing darts at a target with only one big bullseye to hit. It's hard to miss.

For the replacement market, it will mean zero energy-level savings over the model that is likely to be replaced. Refrigerator producers have made steady strides in improving their products' efficiency over the past several decades. A refrigerator's useful life is about 12 to 15 years and a model that old may be 60 percent less efficient than a new replacement, if the buyer chooses the right size and model.

The low-cost choice for the new and replacement market is the classic 18-cubic-foot Energy Star top freezer. It's universally available, simple, dependable and suitable in size for a typical household of two to four people. Chances are it will be 30 to 40 percent more efficient than the refrigerator found in most other homes.

As with clothes washers, a few companies manufacture nearly all refrigerators. They are familiar names like Whirlpool, General Electric, Maytag and Frigidaire and they all make very efficient refrigerators, including one or more 18-cubic-foot Energy Star models, at prices that should be impossible to ignore.

Just the same, the market is doing just that when it comes to the 18-cubic-foot Energy Star top freezer. Buyers have opted for models that are less efficient or that use more energy — and producers have encouraged the trend. Buyers want bigger refrigerators or home builders are giving it to them. With homes larger than in the past, there's more room for them, too, and the bigger they are the more energy they use. Refrigerator size increased regularly in the nineties from an average of under 20 cubic feet to 22 cubic feet a decade later where they remain, even as household sizes have shrunk.

The market is also resisting Energy Star, which requires that refrigerators be 20 percent more efficient that the federal standard. Their market penetration peaked at about a third of all fridges sold in 2005 and drifted down to 31 percent in 2008.

Lastly, there is also a move away from the top freezer. Long the workhorse of refrigerators, it has been losing ground to side-by-side refrigerators, which may be a third less efficient for the same size. The side-by-sides are also at least partially responsible for the size inflation. Top freezers have volumes no bigger than 22 cubic feet, while side-by-sides range several cubic feet larger. They also often have energy-wasteful ice makers in their doors.

Popular culture can't seem to get enough of them, either. They are symbols of the good or, at least, prosperous life and can be found in many popular television shows. In 2010, these included *Desperate Housewives, The Good Wife, Modern Family* and *House,* ensuring their high profile in the market — Kitchen Queen Rachel Ray's standard top freezer model notwithstanding.

The worst trend in refrigerators, though, is the rapid rise of the two refrigerator house. It was up to 22 percent in 2005 and the DOE expected the percentage to rise. The second refrigerator was an antique that remained running in the house — dispatched to renovated basements — when a new one was purchased.

Energy Star offers no resistance to the side-by-side movement. Side-by-side refrigerators earn Energy Star labels even though they often use 200 kilowatt-hours a year more than top freezers. They just need to beat the separate federal standards for side-by-sides — which is not an absolute standard — to get the label.

Bottom freezer models are a third, least-chosen option. Their efficiency is between the top and side-by-side levels, but they too are bigger than the top freezers and are also taking market share away from them.

Manufacturers are pushing the side-by-sides and the bottom freezer refrigerators because they offer better profit margins than the top freezers. Yet, for their greater cost and inefficiency the only advantages they offer are the larger, though unnecessary, size and less bending. Perhaps the only natural market for them are ice tray-challenged homeowners who don't like to bend (or can't) and who have large families — not a big market, but manufacturers have been successful in selling side-by-sides and bottoms to an increasingly larger share of the refrigerator market anyway.

Energy Star top freezer models nevertheless remain plentiful and inexpensive. Eight of the TopTenUSA ranked refrigerators were top freezers, ranging in size from 18 to 22 cubic feet. The cost-effective winner in the winter of 2011 ranked fifth. It was a General Electric 18-cubic-foot model priced then at $500 that used 335 kilowatt-hours a year. The energy savings during a 12-year span before replacing the refrigerator was calculated at $207 or more than enough to make up for any extra cost over a standard model, such as a non-Energy Star Hotpoint model that went for $450 and used 480 kilowatt-hours — a whopping 43 percent more.

Clothes Dryers

Clothes dryers are so much alike that Energy Star doesn't rate them. (Neither does TopTenUSA.) Five out six dryers sold are electric instead of gas so most also have the same power source in common. Most also have the same capacity of about seven cubic feet.

Trends in buying clothes dryers do exist, however, and they are no more a friend of efficiency hunters than they are with refrigerators. Most buyers will buy a match for their washer and it's likely to cost them more money if they don't put the best buy first (though they should be front loaders like their washer mates).

A few energy efficient features are better criteria than color, brand and style. Dryers that have moisture sensors, air dry options and cool down or permapress cycles use less energy and take better care of the clothes. These features are not huge energy savers, but they may come with less expensive models just as well as with high-priced dryers. The cost range for electric dryers can be anywhere from a few hundred dollars to about a thousand dollars.

Another energy saver involves a small cost and revives the practice, in a limited way, of how almost everyone dried their clothes before 1960, when dryer sales took off. It's hanging at least some clothes on a line to dry. However, it wouldn't mean a complete return to days past. Instead of drying clothes outside, they would be dried *inside* — on a small indoor clothes line apparatus. That way, buyers can save money on energy by using their dryers less frequently. They also wouldn't be risking their neighbor's ire or standards on what makes for appropriate backyard views.

One clothesline model can be screwed in against the wall and is guaranteed for ten years, though it could probably last forever. It's good for hanging up straight from the washer all those slow-drying towels, sweat shirts and jeans. Wall-mounted clotheslines sell for around $150. If there is enough space, floor models sell for under $50. It was drying clothes outside his home that made the difference between zero and near zero for architect David Pill's Charlotte, Vermont, house and the indoor setups can be found in home improvement outlets, hardware stores and from other retailers, including those found on the Internet.

Stoves

The oldest member of the household — predating refrigerators, dishwashers, clothes washers and dryers and electric lighting by many hundreds of years — has outlived its usefulness. Stoves are just too big, inefficient and unnecessary. They're mostly empty space spending too much time and energy heating themselves up. A countertop trio of microwave oven, convection toaster oven and range can do the job more cheaply and efficiently in an age where slaving over a hot stove has lost all meaning.

Still, homebuyers expect to see them when they enter the kitchen and they will likely remain a fixture in the home. The default efficiency arrangement is to buy the basic self-cleaning electric stove with a coil-burner range and have a microwave and a convection toaster oven on the countertop. The stove can be called on for cooking the Thanksgiving bird, while the range atop it and the countertop cooking appliances will wind up getting the most use. Energy use could be virtually the same even with the stove in the kitchen and since it won't get much use there's no need to spend much on one. The cost for the three will be less than a typical combination oven/range and microwave unit.

Electric ovens and ranges are in a majority of homes and the basic self-cleaning model is made by most brand-name appliance manufacturers. They can be bought for around $300 — cheaper than the gas version. The price rises if features such as smooth tops and convection heating are added.

Convection ovens are preferred over conventional ovens because they cook food more evenly. However, if the homeowner is buying the convection toaster oven, they're already covered when preparing most meals. If the Thanksgiving bird is a Cornish hen or two, then they'll have one less reason to ever use their big, conventional floor model oven because the hens can easily fit inside the toaster oven.

The prices of both the convection toaster oven and the microwave oven will vary, largely based on size. Small ones (under a cubic foot) can be bought for under $100, while larger ones may cost between $200 and $300.

Lighting

Light emitting diodes (LEDs) are the one energy efficiency breakthrough technology in the home. With the twist of a wrist or a flick of a switch, LED lighting reduces the energy cost of lighting a home by 80 percent from what it costs to use incandescent lighting, the 19th century breakthrough technology LEDs are being designed to replace.

They entered the lighting mainstream in the first decade of the 21st century with a tiny niche product: Christmas lights. Progress was quick, though. By the second decade, they became available to fill general lighting needs in the home and were found on shelves of retailers across the country along with fluorescent and halogen lighting.

The price is what would be expected of a new product. It's high — just as televisions, personal computers and cell phones were when they first entered the mass market — but that's changing.

For years, LEDs were directional lights that had trouble producing the incandescent color and brightness people were used to seeing. By 2010, they got just about everything at least half right.

Most household bulbs are either 60 watts, 75 watts or 100 watts. By 2010 several manufacturers were able to produce 12-watt LEDs that were the equivalent of 60-watt incandescent bulbs in their color and brightness. They could be found wherever light bulbs were sold and on the Internet. Besides being much more efficient, they lasted far longer — 25,000 hours versus less than 1,000. They also lasted much longer than CFLs, which burn for about 8,000 hours, are cooler to the touch and slightly more efficient (CFLs need 13 watts to be the equivalent of a 60-watt incandescent). Another advantage for LEDs is that they don't contain mercury, a toxic substance, which is in CFLs. LEDs can be screwed into every socket that was built for incandescent bulbs and it should be just a matter of time before LED manufacturers do as well with 75-watt and 100-watt bulbs.

LEDs' success is timely. Standard incandescent lights will, by law, soon be consigned to history. Production of the bulbs will cease by 2014 — save for some new, more efficient, much more expensive incandescent bulbs — leaving lighting wide open to LEDs.

Mass production should help bring their prices down even more. Major lighting manufacturers, like Philips and Osram Sylvania, and smaller ones, like Lighting Science, were all selling the 60-watt equivalents by early 2011. Cree has produced a 60-watt LED bulb for use in recessed kitchen lighting. The 75-watt and 100-watt equivalents are expected to catch up to the 60-watt equivalents.

LEDs have already gone through several rounds of price cuts and are selling in some instances at half their original cost. It's not quite down to where it needs to be for a zero energy home already facing pressure on expenses throughout the home and where there are (on average) 45 sockets to fill. Still, it wouldn't be too big a surprise to see them there by 2020, the year zero energy is supposed to go mainstream. With incandescent bulbs off the market and CFLs likely to remain unpopular, LEDs could take over if their price comes down. There are already expectations that a LED bulb could cost just a few dollars — a mainstream, off-the-shelf price that should make for a very bright, energy efficient, non-toxic future in lighting.

10

Sustaining the Drive

Flooring, plumbing and wiring aren't obvious concerns in developing a zero energy home. Whatever choices are made will have mostly an indirect impact on energy consumption. It's the energy used in producing the product, commonly known as the embedded or embodied energy that is the real concern — the less the better, the same as with everything else in the house. The choices made are also important for staying within budget, achieving durability, maintaining the highest indoor air quality and doing what's best for the environment.

Flooring

Trees, grass, clay, sand and wool are some of the natural materials used to make floor coverings. Eight materials — five natural, one synthetic and two mixed — are compared here, including cork, linoleum, bamboo, ceramic tiles, concrete, wood, carpeting and vinyl. The first five are sustainable, as are some woods and carpeting, while vinyl is the one completely synthetic material.

Costs extend over a wide range, from barely over a dollar a square foot to well over $10 a square foot. The difference in price between the cheapest and the most expensive covering, even spread over a home that is hundreds of square feet below the median, could easily reach $10,000 or more.

Laminates, another possibility, are purposely excluded here. While increasingly popular, they are neither cheap nor sustainable. Having two strikes against them is too much. Marble, stone and granite are eliminated too. They're wonderfully natural and widely admired for their durability and attractiveness, but they're terribly expensive and not the type of flooring found in the typical home, zero energy or otherwise.

The eight materials are listed roughly according to their initial cost, including labor and materials. Costs tend to go up from the first (vinyl) to the last (wood), though the prices for a number of flooring types extend over quite a wide range due to quality, durability, composition and other factors. The difference between covering a house with one type of floor and the next one down on the list may be in the hundreds of dollars and thousands jumping from bottom to top. (Some websites, like Green Floors, specialize in sustainable flooring material.)

Vinyl. Flooring made out of vinyl is the cheapest option — the same as when it's used in siding and in window frames. While its price is a big plus, vinyl carries a lot of negative baggage. It's a petroleum-based product laden with toxins. That may not be such a big deal with siding; it's outdoors. But spread out and stomped on daily, vinyl flooring is harmful to indoor air quality.

Vinyl is a thin hard material; laid on a slab foundation it doesn't offer help with insulating the house. Also, great care has to be taken in installing it over the concrete. Vinyl flooring can be damaged by moisture trapped under it. Concrete has to be tested before the flooring is put on top of it. If it's not dry enough, then vinyl flooring shouldn't be used.

Vinyl is also not durable compared to other floor coverings, having one of the shortest life spans — one or two decades — of any of them. Because of that, vinyl is not very cost-effective even with its low initial expense since it will have to be replaced much sooner than many other floor coverings.

Linoleum. Linoleum is the green vinyl. It's another thin, hard material that's easy to install in rolls or tiles like vinyl and that needs to be worked with carefully around moisture. Linoleum begins to separate itself on price. It generally costs more, but shopping around may narrow or eliminate the spread. The big difference is that linoleum is made from linseed oil, pine rosin and other natural products, most of them renewable. It's also biodegradable, recyclable and far more durable than vinyl.

It doesn't undergo a toxic, carbon-emitting, energy intensive manufacturing process either. Much of the raw material is grown naturally rather than synthesized, as is necessary when making vinyl, but considerable energy is expended in transportation. Linseed oil comes from the flax plant, which is mainly found around the eastern Mediterranean region, so either the plant or the linoleum, which is made in Europe, has a long way to go to reach North America.

Carpeting. Carpeting has something for every taste. It's made from natural, synthetic and recycled materials. It's the last that earns carpeting the third spot in the price order. Aside from being inexpensive, recycled carpeting adds some insulation to the foundation (R-2.2 per inch, according to the Radiant Panel Association) and is kinder to falling children and other bodies than linoleum, vinyl and other hard floorings. Recycled carpeting is made of plastic bottles and other manner of materials that would otherwise spend an eternity in landfills. Installing recycled carpeting may virtually be a public service.

Recycled carpeting is not among the most durable floor coverings, though it should outlive vinyl.

Synthetic carpeting is made of nylon. Its characteristics match those of recycled carpeting fairly well, with one big exception. It's not recycled material. It's an original, unsustainable petroleum-based product, though it can be recycled and variations of it may contain recycled content.

Wool is the natural one. It easily adds more insulation value to the ground floor than any other carpeting — or any flooring material for that matter. It has a value of R-3.3 per inch while the hard coverings are one or less. Wool is also the softest and most durable carpet, if not quite as long lasting as sustainable hard flooring, but its advantages come at a price. Wool carpeting is very often the most expensive flooring of any of the ones being considered here. Over the long run — albeit measured in decades — it would be more expensive even than marble, which may never have to be replaced.

Stained concrete. Leaving the foundation bare might leave the house looking unfinished, but staining concrete is an option that gives the foundation the appearance of being covered. It's not a common option and it's not cheap either if done by professionals, as is recommended. Non-toxic stains are available, making staining concrete one of the most, if not the most sustainable, cost-effective choice.

Bamboo. Bamboo is highly sustainable because it's made from a strong, hardy, fast-growing grass ready for harvesting every two to seven years. The final product that's laid down in a home is a very hard, strong surface that can last decades. Bamboo is probably the last of the low-priced options. Given its low cost and high durability, it may be the cost-effective floor covering champ (not counting stained concrete). On the down side,

Bamboo flooring.

DURO-DESIGN FLOORING INC.

Another look in bamboo.

bamboo isn't any help with energy efficiency. Its hard surface reflects heat and sound. Bamboo also loses a little sustainability cachet because of its embedded or embodied energy costs. Bamboo comes from China so it has the highest transportation costs of any flooring being shipped to North America. Its cultivation, harvesting and manufacturing are, at the least, suspect for what resources are used and how they are used. While it's possible to grow bamboo without fertilizers and pesticides, it's hard to know how bamboo is grown in a closed society like China. For the same reason it's also not easy to know what chemicals — specifically, formaldehydes — are used in manufacturing it. Finally, how the workers who raise, harvest and process the bamboo are treated is more of a concern than with the Europeans who produce linoleum flooring.

Cork. Cork or, specifically, agglomerated cork is among the most sustainable and energy efficient choices. It's energy efficient because it helps insulate the home all year round, remaining cool in the summer, warm in the winter. Cork is sustainable because it comes from a renewable resource. Cork is derived from the bark of the cork tree, which is sheared of its bark in much the same way wool is sheared from sheep. The bark grows back on the trees naturally, then is harvested again and again, roughly every 9 years over the life of the tree or about 150 years.

DURO-DESIGN FLOORING INC.

Cork flooring.

The cork is used for, well, corks and agglomerated cork is made from what's left behind. Were it not for cork flooring this might be dumped in a landfill. (Some cork waste goes into linoleum too.)

Cork flooring has many other desirable qualities along with its natural supply lines. It's fire-retardant, resilient, long-lasting, recyclable, doesn't absorb moisture and dust, is resistant to rot and insects, stands up to wear and tear and provides insulation against sound, as well as heat loss. Cork's main disadvantage is its cost. It falls in the middle of the sustainable pack of floor coverings, costing perhaps twice as much as vinyl — or even more — to buy and have installed.

Another disadvantage is cork's embedded energy cost. Transportation costs are high in dollars and carbon emissions — though not quite as high as either bamboo or linoleum. Half the cork comes from Portugal and the rest from several western Mediterranean countries, including Spain, France, Italy, Algeria and Tunisia.

Ceramic tiles. Ceramic tiles are sustainable and energy efficient, though in ways that are different from cork and bamboo. They're made from clay, a natural and widely available material that is easily disposed of or recycled. Ceramic tiles are also energy efficient because they absorb heat from the sun by day and release it at night, lowering heating costs.

They're easy to maintain and will outlive any owner, though if something heavy is dropped on them they will likely crack and need to be replaced. Ceramic tiles also are free of any indoor air quality concerns and are extremely easy to clean.

Cost is one drawback. They typically cost more than cork and can be much more expensive as they come in a wide variety of styles, colors and compositions. There are, for example, five grades of hardness. In most cases, grade three is the right level for home floors. Also, some tiles absorb heat better than others. Both hardness and heat absorbing properties will affect price.

Their embedded energy is relatively high, too, since high heat is needed to make the tiles hard. Ceramic tiles may also have high transportation costs. They're predominately an import, with Italy the number one producer. One other disadvantage is that manufacturers have to control two toxic emissions — fluorine and lead — during manufacturing.

Wood. Hardwood floors will last longer than any of the other floor coverings discussed so far. They're relatively easy to clean and maintain, but they are expensive and not necessarily sustainable. Sustainable wood is either FSC-certified or recycled or reclaimed wood and both of those choices are likely to cost even more — if a source can be found. Neither is widely available. However, in a throwaway society and an era when abandoned housing is common, shopping around may yield reclaimed wood in excellent condition at bargain prices. A number of websites are devoted to linking sellers with buyers across the country (Wood World, Build. Recycle.Net and StickTrade.com are three).

A zero energy home will likely have a mix of flooring, just as traditional homes do, although the mix might be different. It should take into account cost-effectiveness, energy efficiency and sustainability. Linoleum in the kitchen and dining room (if there's a dry foundation under foot) is an easy choice for lean budgets; ceramic tile for more expansive ones. Recycled carpeting in the bedrooms where bare feet tread will work for those lean budgets, while bigger budgets will allow for a more expensive exception in the master bedroom, like cork.

It might be a good idea to save room in any budget for ceramic tiles in the bathrooms. If their total floor area is less than 60 square feet covering them with ceramic tiles wouldn't be that much more expensive than vinyl or linoleum. Installing tiles also avoids any moisture concerns.

That leaves the living room and its 200 to 400 square feet. It could be covered with recycled carpeting, bamboo or cork in less expensive homes and ceramic tile, wool carpeting or FSC or reclaimed wood in higher-priced houses. In a cold-climate zero energy home with a southern exposure with banks of windows, ceramic tiles would have the edge. They'd absorb the sun's heat by day and release it at night. In warmer climates cork might get the nod.

Plumbing

Plumbing is another occasion to be grateful that in developing a zero energy home the gospel is to think small or, at least, smaller. Plumbers are among the highest paid workers in home building and having them do less than more will be rewarded in lower labor costs.

Short, simple lines are also good for making the house more energy efficient. Hot water will lose less heat getting to its destination because it will take less time getting there. Another benefit of the minimalist approach to plumbing is lower supply costs. Shorter and straight is cheaper than long lines at right angles with expensive elbow and other joints in between. Besides having shorter water and waste lines, it also helps to have lines centrally located and as straight as possible.

What carries the water in and the waste out of the house will affect labor costs and energy efficiency, as well as the cost of materials. Indeed, they might be the deciding factors in choosing copper or cross-linked polyethylene (PEX), the two leading choices. Easily discarded from consideration is cast iron and a quartet of plastic piping, including polybutylene, Acrylonitrile Butadiene Styrene (ABS), polyvinyl chloride (PVC) and chlorinated polyvinyl chloride (CPVC). All five lose out on cost, durability and environmental grounds.

Copper. Copper tubing or pipes have been used to carry water going back to ancient Egyptian times. It's had competition over time (remember lead?), but over the last century copper has been the material plumbers work with most. It is durable, strong, malleable and highly sustainable. It's a naturally occurring element and easily recycled. Copper also resists corrosion and bacteria, a good thing for a pipe carrying drinking water.

For many years, copper was also inexpensive. That changed in 2005, when its price skyrocketed, collapsed and then soared to new heights within five years. Copper's price during this period hit peaks that were several times the price of PEX. Copper prices' volatility suggests the possibility that eventually there will be no contest with PEX at all. PEX will win. Demand for copper in wiring — see the next section and the following chapter — is only likely to grow and copper might easily price itself out of the plumbing competition before becoming cheap again. Still, copper is very much in the game for the foreseeable future, while cost may remain just one of its biggest disadvantages.

Copper isn't energy efficient either. Hot water running through copper pipes is going to lose heat. Insulation for the pipes is recommended, but that's another cost. Copper creates some environmental problems too. Copper smelting results in the emission of dangerous wastes like sulfuric acid.

Cross-Linked Polyethylene. PEX was first used in North America in the eighties after being used in Europe for more than a decade. Its chief advantage over copper is that it's cheaper to buy, transport and work with. Pipes and tubing made with PEX bend so they don't need as many joints, bringing down labor and material costs. Shipping is lower because instead of stiff pipes of various lengths PEX comes in standard rolls of tubing.

PEX has other advantages as well. It insulates hot water running through it so it loses less heat than water running through copper. It's better at low temperatures too because it won't burst in cold weather, as copper pipes might. PEX also wins on taste. It can't give water a metallic taste nor does it raise health concerns the way dissolved copper does. Also, water flows quietly through PEX, never making the noises heard when it runs through copper.

The main disadvantage of PEX compared to copper is that it's plastic and not biodegradable or recyclable. Two other disadvantages are that it

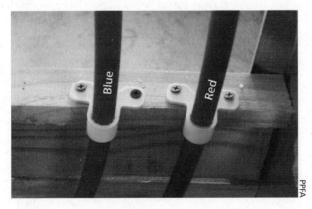

PEX tubing; blue (left) for cold water and red for hot.

Pex tubing in white for hot, cold and waste water.

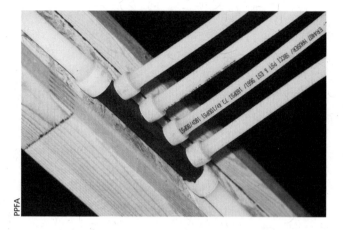

can't be used outdoors and PEX tubing is susceptible to permeation by outside contaminants.

It's quite a stark contrast. Copper is costly and sustainable; PEX is neither. Copper still leads. The 2005 Annual Builder Practices Survey from the National Association of Home Builders (NAHB) indicates that 41 percent of new homes are equipped with copper pipe, and only 19 percent have PEX, but PEX is "attracting growing attention from homebuilders, designers, and trade contractor," according to a 2007 Department of Housing and Urban Development report in *HUD USER* despite lingering ill-deserved association with other less successful plastic plumbing.

In one of the many memorable scenes in *The Graduate* a character goes to some lengths, literally, to deliver one word of advice to the film's young protagonist: "Plastics . . . There's a great future in plastics." Plastics could not live up to the import it was given in that great comic scene. Nor is it worthy of being demonized as some environmentalists would have it. The material has its uses. In January 2009 California, which is generally conceded to have the highest environmental standards of any state, approved the use of PEX.

Wiring

A home's electrical wiring is easy to overlook as a source for energy savings. It's hidden in the walls silently going about its business of transporting electricity, but in doing its job it's likely to be wasting energy.

Electricity and resistance go hand in hand. Resistance creates unwanted heat and wasted electricity. Using thicker wires over as short a distance as possible will lead to lower resistance and higher energy efficiency than found in most homes. Thicker copper wires will cost more money, but the savings from lower resistance and from using less wire will make up the extra cost within a few years.

Typical building codes allow homes to be built using 14 AWG (American Wire Gauge, which is a measure of wire thickness). The thicker the wire, the less resistance the electricity flowing through it encounters. Fourteen is thick enough to keep the wire from heating up so much that it's likely to cause a fire, but it doesn't address efficiency. Lower sizes — the next is 12 AWG — are better in most cases. They are especially more efficient where the wires lead to high energy users, like clothes dryers and hot water heaters. Lower gauges also help improve the performance of some appliances, like the sound quality of stereo equipment.

The length of wiring is dependent on the size of the house and the number of rooms. The smaller the house the less wire will be used. Sockets are generally installed in the wall every six feet, a tradition well worth observing, as the next chapter surely shows.

11

More Stuff

A house is just a pile of stuff with a cover on it. You can see that when you're taking off in an airplane. You look down, you see everybody's got a little pile of stuff. All the little piles of stuff. And when you leave your house, you gotta lock it up. Wouldn't want somebody to come by and take some of your stuff. They always take the good stuff. They never bother with that crap you're saving. All they want is the shiny stuff. That's what your house is, a place to keep your stuff while you go out and get ... more stuff!

— George Carlin

ONE OF THE LEGENDARY COMEDIAN's classic routines, *Stuff* becomes even more relevant with the passing decades. Homeowners are stuffing their homes with the good stuff, the shiny stuff, the stuff powered by electricity.

The trend is particularly fierce in electronics. The number of televisions, computers and other electronic equipment in the home is going up fast. A zero energy home may be just another energy efficient home a few years down the road if its owners load it up with electrical stuff at the same pace consumers have been doing.

For decades, having at least one color television set in the home was a given — in over 99 percent of homes. Now the *number* of sets in each house has increased, and at a much faster rate than the population has. In 2001, 44 percent of the 63 million single-family homes had 3 or more sets. Four years later, that was up to 68 percent of 72 million.

Computers swung up too. In 2005, desktop computers were in 75 percent of single-family homes, up from 65 percent 4 years earlier. The jump in homes with 2 or more was even greater, to 28 percent from 11 percent.

Homeowners were also buying more stuff that is connected to televisions and computers. For example, the number of single-family homes with printers rose to 68 percent from 60 percent of the total over the same period.

As the number of electronic gadgets have increased in the home, so too has the amount of energy they use and their share of total electric use. They used 11 percent of electricity in 2006 compared to 7 percent in 2001. It's expected to keep on growing, too. US energy use from televisions and computer equipment — most of the home electronic use and also a majority of all plug-in use — is expected to increase 3.5 percent annually through 2025, to more than double the level of consumption in 2003 — a rate far faster than population growth.

World growth will be even greater. Energy used by computers and consumer electronics will triple by 2030, according to a 2009 International Energy Agency study. In addition to televisions, desktops, cell phones and printers used in the home, the study also included laptops, DVD players and recorders, modems, set-top boxes, portable telephones, answering machines, game consoles, audio equipment, clocks, battery chargers and children's games.

Home electricity use is increasing too, the report says, and the growth in consumer electronics is the reason why. Globally, the report says consumer electronics account for close to 15 percent of total residential electricity consumption.

Electricity use worldwide may be even higher if plug-ins, like those mentioned at the end of this chapter, are included. For example, a survey of Wisconsin homes found that plug-ins accounted for between 15 and 30 percent of the residential electricity used in the state.

Any chance of reducing or even slowing down the amount of energy used in homes by consumer electronics and other plug-ins will depend on a number of factors that include energy efficiency, size, number of units, type of technology and hours of use. The possible combinations are staggering for televisions and computers and they'll have the biggest impact of all the electronic equipment when it comes to whether or not a home reaches zero year in and year out. After all, if electronic usage trends continue, a homeowner that has not paid anything for utilities after living in their new home for a year may well start getting one in the future — possibly an ever-growing bill too.

Televisions

Where TVs were small boxy picture tubes for decades, they are now large flat screens. Three different types compete for consumer dollars: liquid crystal displays (LCDs), plasma and rear projection.

LCD uses less energy than the other two. LCD sets have the edge over them because they are generally smaller. They are also simply much more energy efficient than the plasma sets, as are the rear projection models. The size spread, however, is decreasing — another sign of a big is better arms race as much a part of the television story as the flattening of the set.

Starting at under 20 inches, television screens now reach to over 80. The spread in size is matched by the range of energy use and price. Televisions cost from under $200 to several thousand dollars and use anywhere from as little as 50 kilowatt-hours or less to over 1,000 kilowatt-hours annually (based on being on 5 hours a day).

One of the more interesting developments in television energy efficiency is that LCDs are both becoming more energy efficient and using more energy at the same time. This is because manufacturers are switching to producing sets that are back lit by light-emitting diodes (LEDs) instead of fluorescent lighting. LEDs create a better picture. They also don't contain mercury, as does fluorescent lighting, but they're also the reason that LCDs are able to compete on size better with the other two screen technologies. So while the amount of energy per inch goes down on LCD, the amount of LCD LED-backlit energy used increases with size.

With the number and size of televisions increasing, they easily have the potential to dwarf the energy use of any major appliance because of the amount of energy they use, the time they are used for and their (average) three to one numerical advantage over major appliances in the home.

However, since there are sets on the market that use very little energy, it should be easy to turn to Energy Star to find them. Just as with refrigerators, though, to be eligible for listing, a set just needs to be more efficient than other televisions of its kind, not better than all kinds. The result is that there are Energy Star televisions that draw down over 400 kilowatt-hours annually — more than many Energy Star refrigerators. Add a couple more television energy hogs, which in total would suck up as much energy as the entire kitchen, and it would be difficult to imagine a house equipped with three big televisions not having any utility bills.

It is however, possible to locate energy-sipping televisions. Again, the TopTenUSA rankings provide the help. TopTenUSA divides televisions up into small, medium and large categories. Not surprisingly, LED-backlit LCD televisions fill every spot.

The small category, which would have been large a generation ago, has an abundance of cheap kilowatt-sipping models made by little known

One of the most energy efficient televisions and, as promoted here, backlit by LED.

companies selling for under $300. The fourth-ranked 24-inch LED-backlit AOC model using just 50 kilowatt-hours annually had the lowest price, at $230. Vizio had four models in the top ten. It's a new company fast becoming known for knocking out cheap televisions. Vizio's lowest priced model in the rankings was a fifth-ranked 22-inch LED-backlit model selling for $280 and using just 43 kilowatt-hours annually. Seventh-ranked Panasonic was the lowest-priced name brand entry. It had a 32-inch LED-backlit model selling for $350 that used 93 kilowatt-hours annually.

The medium-sized category told pretty much the same story. Vizio and Panasonic models stood out again — despite lackluster ranking. Fourth-ranked Vizio had a 37-inch LED-backlit model selling for $588 that used 70 kilowatt-hours annually, while ninth-ranked Panasonic had a 37-inch LED-backlit set selling for $411 that used 122 kilowatt-hours annually.

In the large category, the number one ranked television truly lived up to its lead position. Samsung, which pioneered LED backlighting, ran away from the crowd in price and energy use — using half the kilowatts and costing from hundreds to over a thousand dollars less than the rest of the pack. It was an $897 46-inch set using just 93 kilowatt-hours annually.

Nevertheless, searching Energy Star can also be worthwhile. For example, scanning the list of 835 models uncovered a 19-inch high-definition Hitachi set with LED backlighting using an Energy Star low 25 kilowatt-hours annually. That was just half the search, though. Finding the best price for it was next. A web search came up with one selling for $180 at Radio Shack that received a four and a half star rating from several reviewers.

In the end, the cheapest, fastest way to outfit a zero energy home with televisions is to remember four words: Fewer! Smaller! Energy Star!

Computers

Energy Star also lists computers that may be between 30 percent and 65 percent more efficient than standard computers, depending on how they're used. Finding the most energy efficient computers is both easier and more difficult than with televisions. It's easier because computers are not lumped together. Desktops and notebooks and laptops are listed separately. They are also divided up into performance categories, from least to greatest — four for desktops (A to D); three for laptops (A to C).

The Energy Star computer listing is more difficult because there are so many more to choose from — for both desktops and laptops. Laptops totaled over two thousand, while desktops covered over a thousand, and comparing them is complicated. A complaint made about Energy Star is that the program should toughen standards before too many products qualify. As well, computers may be configured differently and wind up spreading across two, three or four categories, muddying exactly how energy efficient a computer may be compared to other ones.

Desktops top out at over 300 kilowatt-hours annually. In homes with two of these powerful computers, it's like adding — in terms of energy consumption — one of the largest Energy Star side-by-side refrigerators to the house. Zero energy home developers may want to head straight to the laptops. They use a third or less as much energy as Energy Star desktops and laptops in general have become increasingly popular as their prices have fallen significantly.

Matching the Energy Star list with what's available for sale at stores and online isn't easy. Models come and go. Differences are not obvious. After all, they look pretty much alike (they're all boxes of reasonably the same size) and buyers have to be careful to see that model numbers match up precisely. Also, monitors *are* lumped together on their own list: LED, fluorescent and the occasional plasma.

Again, though, TopTenUSA provided an easier way. It had rankings for desktops, laptops and monitors, both large and small, though in the desktop listing the computers may have monitors just as the laptops do. If the site is still in service at the time of this reading, it should be the first stop. Not that it's perfect. It listed some computers that were only available to businesses and other non-retail buyers, and didn't always list prices.

Among TopTen laptops, a third-ranked $310 Acer Aspire model with one gigabyte of memory and a 10-inch screen used 14 kilowatt-hours annually. In the listing of desktops, a third-ranked $465 eMachine model with a monitor used a total of 50 kilowatt-hours annually. It had one gigabyte of memory and an 18.5-inch flat screen. Among monitors the top-ranked model was manufactured by I-Inc. It was a 16-inch LED backlit monitor selling for $80.

Less powerful computers and smaller monitors — using less energy — have dominated the TopTen rankings. Buyers wanting bigger, better ones will have to muddle through the Energy Star listings — and accept that they'll use more energy. For example, a Dell Optiplex (2.93GHz processor speed, 16GB memory) without a monitor used 212 kilowatt-hours.

Overloading

Given modern reality, the amount of energy televisions and computers use doesn't stop with their own consumption. They virtually breed other electronic devices besides the requisite monitor attached to desktops.

Energy Star has lists for a number of them. They include DVD players, printers, faxes and battery chargers and set-top boxes. The last are the 160 million vampires of electrical consumption in the US that remain on even when their hosts are off, sucking more power when they're not being used than when they are.

Taken as a group, buying Energy Star versions can produce significant energy savings. Its blue label combined with the right price tag may be all that any buyer needs to see before deciding to put down their money. Any more effort for any buyer without an abiding interest in electronics is likely to be an inefficient use of time and energy.

Electric devices that offer convenience, such as assisting in doing work that would otherwise be done manually, are also tough fits in zero energy homes. They tap little energy, but then there probably isn't any left to use if a house is going to produce as much as it consumes. They include electric can openers, screwdrivers, toothbrushes, pencil sharpeners, staplers, knives, blankets, window shades, shoe polishers, cheese graters, egg timers, jar openers, nose trimmers, cat litter boxes, dog doors and other optional electricity-using stuff that isn't even shiny or in need of being locked up.

12

Under Its Own Power

JOHN SUNDE WAS A PIONEER OF ZERO ENERGY DEVELOPMENT, the kind President Jimmy Carter would have loved. He used very little energy in his modest suburban Brentwood, New York, split-level ranch, not because he was energy efficient, but because he used very little energy.

Sunde conserved energy by not having any air conditioning or clothes dryer. He dried his clothes outside on a clothesline and, in winter, might carry a portable space heater to whatever room he was going to stay in rather than use his oil-fueled boiler. He had one television and one computer and used his dishwasher sparingly. In two stages during 1998 and 1999, Sunde covered all of one side of his roof and much of the other with solar panels and wiped out his electricity bill.

Conservation may have gone the way of Jimmy Carter's cardigans, but Sunde was way ahead of his time with solar panels. Connecting a system like his 7.4 kilowatts to the utility grid was exceedingly rare. Less than a thousand homeowners across the US followed his lead in connecting any photovoltaic systems to the grid in 2000.

Within a few years though, a minor rush was on and American homes equipped with photovoltaic installations linked to the grid have become one of the fastest growing sources of electric power anywhere. In 2004, 5,000 were installed and by 2009 over 30,000 — despite it being one of the worst years financially for homeowners and developers in history.

Not only did more homeowners buy, they also bought bigger. From 2000 to 2009, the size of the average residential system increased from two kilowatts of power to over five kilowatts. By 2010, grid-connected solar arrays had been installed at some 100,000 residences and were producing about 500 megawatts of photovoltaic power or about the amount from a typical coal-burning power plant. No longer was solar the purview of tree huggers living in off-the-grid homes far from urban centers. They were on the house on the way to the commuter train station, just down the block or maybe even next door. It was a small, but national retail business that brought in several billion dollars in sales in less than a decade.

Solar or photovoltaic had taken the leap zero energy homes needed if they were ever going to make it into the mainstream. As with spray-in insulation, triple pane windows and tankless water heaters, solar had established a track record, however slight, of production, sales, delivery, installation and performance with retail consumers across the country. In short, it was marketable.

Solar equipment can be bought off the shelf at the mall or over the Internet, but purchasing solar equipment is not the recommended way to get solar panels up on the roof of a home. Hiring experienced professionals is — and they supply the panels or modules and other equipment. It costs more this way, but even production home builders will typically hire subcontractors who specialize in solar installations to do the job.

Installing solar panels requires special tools, skills and insurance if the job is to be done right, with the least amount of worry and material cost. Climbing up onto a roof, along with hoisting heavy solar panels and connecting them to the grid, is not without risk to body and property. (Seeing a ladder with a motorized hoist used to carry the hefty panels up to the roof should reassure homeowners that hiring someone else to do the job was a smart choice.)

Finding an experienced, competent and reputable solar installer may be all that's necessary. They will tell the buyer what they will get out of the system — and even if they should get the system at all. For example, they

Brentwood, Long Island home with solar panels, facing west with more panels on the roof's eastern slope.

may tell a prospective buyer that the roof of the house they are building or already own won't receive enough sunlight to make installing any photovoltaic panels worthwhile. (As an alternative to staring at the roof from sunrise to sunset with notebook and pencil in hand, they have tools that tell them how much sunlight a surface gets during a day. One is the Solar Pathfinder, retailing for around $300.)

Still, when buying something that may cost as much as a mid-sized sedan, it's good to be an informed consumer. It will help in selecting the right installer. Among the things that count when buying solar electric systems is knowing the right size, its cost, the parts of the system, the amount of sunlight it will receive, financial incentives, local utility rates and the environmental benefits.

Getting It All Together
INSTALLERS

Homeowners or developers looking for installers can find them on the Internet. One of the easiest searches would be on the website of the North American Board of Certified Energy Practitioners (NABCEP). It

specializes in certifying solar electric and thermal installers and their certified installers can be found in most states and in Canada.

California, the biggest, most sophisticated solar market by far, encour-
ages anyone applying for its solar financial incentives to use installers certified by NABCEP. The state had the most installers — over 200 at the
end of 2010 — while Colorado was second with over 100. In those two
states, plus a dozen or so more, it should be easy enough to find several
NABCEP-certified installers to choose from within a reasonable driving
distance of most homes.

Electricians and other professionals with solar installation experience
are other possibilities. Some states or utilities may require approved installers — sometimes licensed electricians — for anyone applying for rebates.
Whoever the candidates may be, there should be several of them. They
must be licensed, bonded, experienced, give free estimates and be able to
provide contact information for several customers that will recommend
their work.

SIZE

A three-kilowatt system may be too big for some homes; seven too small.
Still, if builders and buyers developed the home using passive design and
made it as energy efficient as possible, installing a system within the range
of three to seven kilowatts will produce as much energy as the house uses,
more or less.

It helps that installers are experienced with installing systems within
that range. Five kilowatts is the national average and a number of zero
energy efforts have similar-sized systems (though the size link appears
only coincidental). Below three and the price per watt may rise as the project loses its economy of scale for the installer. Above seven and the home
has been built too big, too inefficiently or the system is producing too little
power, which may be attributed to the amount of sunshine it receives, how
it was installed or both.

PRODUCTION

Not all kilowatts are equal. The location of a home, the orientation and tilt
of the panels and other factors will make a significant difference in how

much sunlight hits a solar panel array and is converted into electricity during the course of a year. The more sun the system gets, the more electric power it produces and the fewer kilowatts buyers need to purchase to supply the kilowatt hours their central air conditioning, refrigerators, lights and every other user of electricity in the house consumes.

Typically, most of the US and Canada would get over 1,000 kilowatt hours annually out of a single fixed south-facing one-kilowatt solar panel installation. Another way of looking at it is that an installation with just one third of a kilowatt of power could produce enough kilowatt hours to operate an Energy Star refrigerator for a year (if all the energy it produced could be stored first).

Some locations are considerably more fortunate than others. The sunny Southwest can get over 1,600 kilowatt hours from a one-kilowatt system, while some northern spots may dip under 1,000 kilowatt hours. Yet even the grimmest northern cities get more sun than most of northern Europe, where 800 kilowatt hours is not uncommon. That means some Southwestern residents can do just as well with a three-kilowatt system as many Northern Europeans could do with a system twice as big.

Orientation is another solar production changer. Facing south supplies about 25 percent more electricity than east and west and more than twice as much as north.

The tilt of the panels also matters. Having a system that follows the sun is the ideal. It could improve production by over a third. However, systems that follow the sun, or at least can be adjusted up or down, are likely to be unappealing on several counts. They cost more, take time, effort and money to operate and maintain and they are likely to look less attractive to owners and neighbors alike.

Some homeowners or developers may be in better positions than others regarding tilt. The classic adobe home with its flat roof — something else Southwestern residents have in abundance — affords greater access to roofs for adjusting the tilt. Elevated or lowered — fifteen degrees in winter and summer, respectively, from their spring and fall position — panels will generally be out of sight.

Still, a fixed system mounted flat against the roof has one almost irresistible attraction. A solar installation's optimum angle is the same in degrees as the home's latitude, which is roughly the same as the pitch of many gabled roofs. Indeed, it couldn't be much neater: in North America the further north a house is located, the steeper the pitch of its roof (the better to lose snow, as well as catch sun).

Homeowners unsure of whether fixed or moveable is best for them should discuss it with their installer. One alternative is to add more panels to a fixed system. It might get as much or more sun for less money than a smaller adjustable installation.

The wiring, inverter efficiency and other factors also affect production. The National Renewable Energy Laboratory's PVWatts calculator enables anyone to calculate exactly how much in cities all over the world simply by pointing and clicking. They can replace the default numbers (from a southern tilt to any other) to draw a profile of their own situation.

SOLAR PANELS

To look at them, panels are fairly indistinguishable from one another. They're all blue-black slick-faced rectangles. The most common are made of mono- and polycrystalline silicon. They don't have a standard size, but they're likely to be in the range of from about 175 watts to 225 watts. At the midpoint, they'll weigh in at about 40 pounds and measure about 3 feet by 5 feet. Panels are mounted on metal frames attached to the roof and barring trees falling on them are good for 25 years, so say the warranties.

A couple of alternatives exist. One is called thin-film solar, which is produced in panels or flexible sheets. It's a newer product that was supposed to take over the solar market.

With solar panels, efficiency and price track each other closely. The more efficient a solar electric collector is the more it costs. The crystalline family is the most efficient and most expensive, with mono costing more than poly. Thin-film is cheaper and less efficient, but its efficiency was supposed to gain on the crystallines while the price stayed down and the savings would be passed onto the consumer — or at least, that was the idea. However, while it has been priced competitively, it's still a work in progress and so takes up more space to catch the same amount of sun. Some roofs may just not have the space and the roof of a zero energy home in particular shouldn't have that much room. (SunPower and Sanyo are the leaders in efficiency. Both produce mono-crystalline panels.) Also, the leading thin-film solar material carries a heavy burden inside. It contains cadmium, one of six infamous hazardous substances recognized world-wide. (A less well-known thin-film, which is known by its acronym, CIGS, contains no cadmium.)

Solar shingles, the other alternative, are only worthwhile for anyone interested in a solar installation that looks good rather than performs well. They're smoothly integrated into the roof with all the other shingles as opposed to mounted on supports attached to the roof's surface. Since they are part of the roof, there is nowhere for the sun's heat to go once it hits the shingles and that hurts their performance, whereas there's a couple of inches of air space between panel mounts and the roof so the heat is dissipated. Choosing shingles also limits the choice of roofs: no steel or tiles, mostly just asphalt. They're also a bit shinier and darker than the asphalt, giving the roof a kind of spotted look that in the end may not be so attractive after all.

Installers may have a particular brand of panel or module they use because they've established a good financial and service relationship with the distributor. This is not a problem. The Florida Solar Energy Center (FSEC) has certified nearly 100 solar panels, so there's plenty to pick from. It may be a problem if the installers under consideration favor panels not on the list.

If each installer contacted uses FSEC-certified panels, shoppers may want to lean towards installers that only use solar panels produced in the US or Canada. This isn't "Buy American" (or Canadian) jingoism. Indeed, they may just as easily be produced here by foreign companies like Sharp (Japanese) or SolarWorld (German). The point is that many companies, wherever they may be headquartered, manufacture good panels, but buying ones made in the US means less fossil fuel is used in transporting the panels, lowering the amount of embedded energy in the products.

INVERTERS

Solar panels produce direct current (DC) electricity. Homes use alternating current (AC). An inverter is a meter-sized metal box between the panels and the home's utility meter that converts DC to AC and is the only

IDEAL HOMES

Solar inverter wired directly to a house's utility meter.

other part of the system, not counting the wiring. California's Go Solar website has a long list of what they call "eligible" inverters. Name brands mix with lesser known inverters. Anyone hiring an installer should expect to find that the inverter the installer is using is on the list.

PAPERWORK

Maybe the best part of leaving the work to installers, is having them do the paperwork, particularly whatever is required to hook up to the grid. It can be an involved process in some states, so much so that installers may need an employee experienced and willing to spend a lot of time on the job doing it.

What Will It Cost?

Solar electric has become much more affordable thanks to severe economic twists and turns. Led by Germany and Japan, world demand started rising around 2000, followed by a flood of products from old and new suppliers.

When the Great Recession hit, demand slumped and prices fell with it. Retail prices for solar panels or modules dropped 45 percent from 2001 to 2011 in both the US and Europe. At the end of that period the average price per watt had headed south of $3.50 a watt from $5.50 in the US.

Residential buyers can get an idea of how much the installer is going to charge them for the entire job by doubling the per watt figure and multiplying that number, in this case $7.00, by how many watts they're considering buying. For example, the cost of the averaged-sized five kilowatt residential system would average around $35,000. (Solarbuzz, an Internet site following the solar industry, surveys the monthly retail price of how much a watt costs.)

By 2011, some major builders were offering optional solar installations and charging only for the panels. Prices were even below retail rates. It is too early to tell what impact this will have on overall costs for solar installations, but it could only come as welcome news for home buyers.

At some point during the life of the panels, the inverter will have to be replaced. They cost from two to three thousand dollars in 2011, but that's it for costs. Operating and maintenance expenses are likely to be minor, though owners should have some way of keeping their sun catchers free and clear of dirt, leaves, twigs and snow.

FINANCIAL INCENTIVES

The cost of solar installations very often may be discounted thanks to various financial incentives, as discussed in Chapter 6. The history has been spotty, though, changing significantly on the national and local level from year to year.

In 2009 the federal government set up a 30 percent discount in the form of a tax credit for 8 years, but buyers need to check with DSIRE to see what, if anything, is available from their state and local governments and utilities. Installers may know only in so far as they can be assigned the cash value directly.

Note that the smaller systems invariably get the highest percentage discount because there are virtually always limits to rebates and other incentives. Some stop at a dollar amount, while others may limit the kilowatts, with five or ten a common ceiling. In some states and the service area of some utilities, buyers were able to get more than half off the cost of a solar installation for over a decade beginning in the nineties. In most states though, the discounts are negligible or nothing.

What's It Worth?

Homeowners buy solar installations primarily for financial reasons. The environment is secondary. The environmental reasons are, however, easy to grasp, indisputable and go well beyond mitigating global warming. The economics are tricky though. Success may depend as much, if not more, on the amount of electricity the system feeds into the grid than is used in the home.

UTILITY RATES

Solar buyers can't begin to know how much their production is worth, how much they'll save and when— if ever — they'll recoup their costs until they know their utility rates and understand their state's or utility's net metering and interconnection policies, if any.

Electric utility rates run to extremes. Indeed, their range is even greater than the amount of sunshine shining from one place to another. At the end of 2010, the highest electric utility rates (Hawaii) were more than three times the lowest (Idaho).

In a perfect grid marriage, that's all that would be needed. The customer would only have to multiply their production by the utility rate to figure out much the solar power they produced was worth and how much they'd be saving — for the first year. If, as expected, utility rates rise over the system's lifetime, then the value — as measured in utility bill savings — will increase over the years. In a zero energy home, the savings will grow while the bill will not. It will always be zero (assuming the owners don't add more electronic devices to their home).

In some states, it is that simple. What isn't used flows directly into the grid of the local utility the home is hooked up to and is recorded, read and credited to the customer's account. When the customer needs electricity, but isn't producing any, they tap the utility's power and their bank of credits (their unused production that the customer fed into the grid). In a zero energy home, the net usage is zero over the course of a year.

In many states it is more complicated and less rewarding than that. Many utilities charge high fees for connecting to the grid or won't pay full retail rates for every watt produced. They may pay wholesale rates, known as the avoided cost, so a zero energy homeowner may still have a bill to pay, besides the utility's monthly administrative charge. Utilities may limit the amount they will buy or, in several states, buy nothing at all because there's no way of connecting to the grid, which means the homeowner without storage capacity will lose what they don't use.

The Interstate Renewable Energy Council (IREC) started grading states on net metering and interconnection in 2006 in an annual report called "Freeing the Grid." In its first few years, few states received As. Most earned Cs, Ds, Fs or no grade at all, because they didn't have any statewide net metering.

CALCULATING THE RETURNS

Calculators available on the Internet allow anyone to crunch the numbers to see what they get in return, financially, for investing in solar power production. The Clean Power Estimator is among the most popular. It's available on websites belonging to the California Energy Commission, the New York State Energy Research and Development Authority (NYSERDA), the Connecticut Clean Energy Fund and Sharp, the electronics company. BP Solar and Kyocera, both major solar panel manufacturers, also have versions on the web.

All that needs to be done is to plug in a zip code and the calculator does the rest. The Estimator is laid out a little differently from one site to another, but the numbers are crunched the same way on each site. The Estimator takes into account nearly every variable: size, price per kilowatts, utility rates, net metering compensation, solar production, interest rates and much more.

When the calculator is opened, there are generally default numbers, but they can all be changed to personalize the numbers. Connecticut's version gets special kudos for nifty graphics, including transforming the number of kilowatts plugged into the program into a photo simulating what the equivalent in panels would look like on the roof of a house. The downside of Connecticut's calculator (and the other states'), at least from the perspective of anyone outside them, is that one of their zip codes or towns are needed to get things started. Not so for Sharp and the solar producers.

The National Renewable Energy Laboratory has its own calculator it calls In My Backyard. It's also good for any locale, but it's not as easy to use and doesn't go into the necessary detail the Estimator does. For example, the utility rates are fixed.

Overall, buying a solar installation is money well spent. The long-term fall in prices is putting systems right for a zero energy home within reach of more and more homeowners and developers. It then becomes a matter of when the expense will be recovered, not if. Developers of zero energy homes with few if any production advantages may still recover their costs, though it might not happen until it's time to replace the panels.

Solar may even be a good business for those homeowners who live in hospitable environments for it. They just might wind up earning a net gain after a few years. In that case, the investment returns are in the double digits. In some states, some of the return can be in the form of cash, not just savings on the utility bill.

Making A Difference

Solar offers a huge benefit, even if it doesn't directly help the homeowner. It is, in fact, more of a gift to the nation's infrastructure and environment that can be summed up in three words: *Free real estate!*

Roofs are free real estate that can be used to harness free energy delivered free every day. This distributed generation linked to the grid and its central generation facilities (the utilities) would provide a number of very important benefits if employed on a large scale, in millions of homes. They include:

1. Residential solar electric reduces the utilities' need to acquire land for solar farms and transmission. Open space is saved, with fewer scars in the landscape from constructing transmission lines across the country. The best transmission line is the one that's never built. Also, utility rates would rise more slowly because of fewer costs to pass on to the customer.
2. Residential solar electric makes supplying all electricity more energy efficient. About eight percent of the electricity supplied by utilities through

long-distance transmission is lost. Relatively none is lost from the distributed generation since the production is done on site at the home.

3. Residential solar electric lowers demand and minimizes congestion in the grid during peak times during the day, when the solar system does all its work, reducing the risks of blackouts and brownouts. In fact, the 2003 Northeast blackout could have been prevented if 80,000 more homes had been equipped with solar electric installations.

4. Residential solar electric reduces the grid's vulnerability to terrorism because of the steady supply of electricity from the home installations during the day.

5. Residential solar electric is a simple way to expand and improve the grid. The grid infrastructure is incredibly outdated and badly in need of repair, but it's complicated and costly work.

A Word About Wind

A home wind power system is a good alternative to solar, but even if they gave away the systems, it would be useful in just a limited number of homes. Only about ten percent of all residences — mostly rural — have enough open windy space surrounding them that'll produce sufficient energy from the wind to light up, heat and cool even the most energy efficient home the way it can be done with solar.

Even then, homeowners could face challenges or outright bans to building them in many communities. There are zoning laws and wind turbines are not allowed in the paths of migratory birds. In a number of states, lawsuits have been filed contesting turbine noise, vibrations, lost property value and even, as in one Michigan case, the reflection of the sun off the spinning blades.

Nor should anyone underestimate the power of NIMBY (Not In My Backyard). In 2011, a Brooklyn neighborhood known as one of the most progressive in the country rose up in protest when just one of several traffic lanes used by cars on a well-traveled street was converted into a bike lane. Imagine the reception a few noisy, giant towers would get there — or elsewhere.

Wind power still has its place. Wind farms in the upper Midwest where the best winds blow and the space for them is available can produce much useful energy. Sea-based wind power sites also appear to have great potential, but distributed wind power in cities and suburbia is a tough sell.

Sunde Topping

In 2010, John Sunde got married. Along with a wife, he got three stepchildren and his first electric bill in a decade. Having already loaded up with solar, he bought $8,500 worth of triple pane Krypton-filled windows and a new boiler system and began educating his new family on energy efficiency to get back to zero.

13

The Ratings Game

LARRY SCHLUSSLER SET OUT TO DEVELOP A ZERO ENERGY HOME on his own in Arcata, California, and no detail however small was going to escape his attention. A year after he moved into his new 960-square foot home on September 21, 2004, he had all the proof he needed that he had succeeded. Twelve months of bills from Pacific Gas & Electric, his utility, added up to a grand total of $59.64 or the utility's charge for his home's connection to its grid. He actually produced 700 kilowatt hours more in that year than he used with just a 1.67 kilowatt solar photovoltaic system.

Not everyone wants to do or is capable of doing what he did. He not only has a Sunfrost, the most energy efficient Energy Star refrigerator, he's the founder and owner of the company that makes it. The same is true for a shower stall he developed that enables him to use a miserly 0.5 gallons of water per minute and still get a good hot shower. He also went to unusual lengths to achieve sustainability and energy efficiency, like using a composting toilet and a goat (though since deceased and not replaced) as a substitute lawn mower and hedge trimmer.

There are ways, though, to get help in developing a sustainable zero energy home from someone other than a builder or contractor. These are

A small home in Arcata, California that produces more energy than it uses.

the independent representatives of rating organizations who can work with the builder, acting as an advocate for reaching zero energy. They'll issue a certificate attesting to how successful the developer of the house has been in reaching zero and how sustainable the house is.

The certification isn't the same as a year of utility bills adding up to zero. Raters are done with their work once the house is built. Certification is more of a marketing tool for developers and homeowners when selling a house. How good it is in boosting sales and resale returns or whether it turns out to be no more than bragging rights won't likely be known for many years to come.

Energy efficiency raters and certifications are plentiful. Quite a few rating systems are good, but only two are widely available and are likely to have enough recognition to be helpful in marketing a house. They're issued under the banner of the Home Energy Rating System (HERS) Index and Leadership in Energy and Environmental Design (LEED) ratings. They're different and yet both offer images and scoring systems that can make zero energy and sustainability more accessible and eye catching for developers and home buyers alike.

A practical twist to the HERS score was introduced by KB Home in 2011. The fifth-largest home builder said every new home would come with an Energy Performance Guide (EPG). In form and substance it was meant to serve the same purpose as miles per gallon (mpg) is when selling cars. The home's estimated monthly gas and electric bill would appear on an EPG sticker. Its calculation was to be based on the house's HERS score, which the house would also come with, appearing in smaller print above the EPG.

An EPG should be more practical than the HERS or LEED because instead of some invented scale it would be a figure in dollar and cents, something everyone could understand. Only at zero would a HERS rating and an EPG mean the same thing. How much of an impact EPG will have is uncertain, but clearly the marketing of ratings is expanding.

Both HERS and LEED standards are free to see on the web. The certifications are not free and that's a drawback, especially for the LEED certification, which can run into the thousands of dollars — many times that of the HERS rating. Still, having HERS, LEED or both ratings done on a house may pay off financially. At least one study has shown a LEED-certified building is worth more than one that isn't and LEED and HERS certification is needed to qualify for some financial incentives. (Yes, check DSIRE.)

HERS

HERS has the right symbolism to make the world more zero-minded. It's not fuzzy. It's specific: a scale reads from 100 to zero with a dial pointing to a home's score with the number over the dial so there's no doubt what level the house has reached. It's easy to read and it's clear that the closer the dial is to zero the more energy efficient the home is.

The scores are calculated by a HERS rater. These are independent consultants who generally score the house twice — once in the planning stages and again when the house is completed. In between, they can be consulted on how to improve the score. They'll also give estimates of energy use, savings and costs, though they are not included in the rating.

Every rater is certified by the Residential Energy Services Network (RESNET). The Oceanside, California-based nonprofit organization has a directory on its website and raters are listed by zip code. A 2009 survey by RESNET found that raters charged anywhere from $165 to $1,000 and averaged $492. If business doubled the average would probably drop by 32 percent to $340. It may have been a prescient survey. The announcement in 2011 by the Pulte Group, the second-largest home builder in the US, and Meritage Homes, the eleventh, as well as KB Home, to have their homes HERS rated could greatly expand the number of houses receiving scores — and lower the cost of getting one.

The HERS standards are basically a comparison test. A home's energy use is compared to how much is used by a reference house the same size and shape and with the same number of bedrooms as the home that's being built. The emphasis is on testing how much its structure and mechanics improve the energy efficiency of cooling and heating space and water. Lighting and appliance energy efficiency is also taken into account, as is any renewable energy power produced on site. Each improvement of one percent is worth a point.

Raters give the house a physical, with, among other things, a blower to test tightness. Data is plugged into software programs and, when everything is done, raters present whoever is paying them a printed certification with a number on a scale, the HERS score. While it's meant to be simple, it is anything but, in no small measure because everything is relative and so little is taken into account. The score is more of a guide than any true measure of energy efficiency and consumption.

The value of a HERS score is largely as a comparison shopping tool. With one number, the shopper knows that the house with the lower score is likely to have a more energy efficient design and more energy efficient insulation, windows and other components. It doesn't necessarily mean the home will use less energy than the one to which it is being compared. Indeed, the picture of a dial moving down a scale with the aim of reaching zero is a little misleading. It is only a projection that the house rated zero will produce as much as it uses, not that it actually will.

In fact, there's a good chance it won't reach zero. What is more likely is that it would take a score of less than zero for the typical family to receive utility bills like the ones Larry Schlussler gets. Nor is this all the uncertainty that surrounds the HERS rating and which only begins to make sense when placed in some context.

Scores are artificially low — and becoming more so — making the home appear more energy efficient than it is. The reference home model is linked to the International Energy Conservation Code (IECC), which is revised every three years. Most states use one of the versions for their building codes. The HERS standard in 2011 was still the equivalent of the 2006 IECC. This makes improving on the reference home and getting a lower score, including zero, easier than it might have been had the reference home been updated. Indeed, by then, California, Florida, New York and a number of other states had bumped their building codes up to the stronger 2009 version.

The 2009 version represented a 15 percent improvement over its 2006 predecessor. Any new houses built in these states would start as a matter of course with a HERS rating of 85 or the equivalent of a 2009 Energy Star home. What was meant to be at least minimally challenging was the new standard in some states.

Scores don't accurately reflect energy use. The scoring doesn't specifically include any energy use (or improvements) attributable to the appliances and other electricity users most people will bring with them on the day they move in or add later. This includes microwaves, televisions, computers, printers, DVDs, video game consoles, toasters and many other plug-in devices. Even some major appliances are left out, like clothes washers and dryers and stoves.

The software may make some allowances for plug-ins, but the scoring is not a measure of the real energy use of whoever occupies the house — especially considering the year that is the software's point of reference. Again, it's 2006 in the software, but real life plug-in energy use is probably higher, since the average plug-in energy use is growing. For example, there can be no accounting for more computers in the house or for recharging e-book readers, iPads and many other gadgets. Electronics and appliances will account for a significant part of electrical usage in the home and not including them in the scoring means actual energy use will be much higher than the rating would indicate.

A Lawrence Berkeley National Laboratory study found that "the agreement between predicted energy cost and actual energy cost was often poor." While the new house uses less energy with the same components as those in the reference home, it often has other components and whether they are efficient or not, they still add kilowatts back in — maybe even more than was saved.

Omissions are not the only way the scoring doesn't reflect actual energy use. The reference house's thermostat settings are set uncomfortably high for most homeowners — 78 degrees in summer — and uncomfortably low — 68 degrees in winter. These settings were a throwback to the oil crisis and government conservation efforts in the Seventies. Whatever their considerable merits, they were resisted then and ever since. Most homeowners prefer a setting somewhere in the middle all year round. For example, a builder may improve a copy of the reference house in every way necessary to obtain a score of zero, but if the homeowner sets the thermostat at 73 degrees year-round in a four-seasons climate, that house will consume more electricity than it produces.

A lower score can lead to more, not less energy being used. The bigger the house and the more sides it has, the more energy it takes to heat and cool. That should count for something in scoring, such as including a penalty for size, but there isn't one. A big house is measured up against a reference house the same size so they can have as good a chance of showing improvement as a small house. Yet it's easier to improve the energy efficiency of a big house — and its score — than a small home. This can be explained by the fact that because the smaller house uses less energy for heating and cooling, the amount of energy used to heat water "becomes a larger relative component in the final rating score," according to a study by the US Green Building Council.

If developers of smaller houses have to work harder and spend more money to get the same scores, it'll discourage the building of smaller houses — even though the smaller homes would likely use less energy. The advantage may switch to the small house developer striving for a HERS 0 however. The big home may have a lower score up to the final stage, but because it's using more energy it will need a larger solar installation to earn enough points to reach zero. Still, energy efficiency is just a means to the end, which is using less energy, and a big house point penalty is still necessary.

It's easier to get a low score in the south than in the north. Energy efficiency gains are easier in warmer areas than colder areas because the total heating and cooling load is lower and they don't need as much insulation to get better scores. That's not, strictly speaking, a flaw in the HERS system. Still it undermines its credibility.

A HERS 0 home is a worthy goal and achievement under any circumstances. Still, it would be even better if lower energy use were given greater weight. This would not transform HERS into a panacea for wasteful energy use, no more so than a 100 miles per gallon sticker on a compact will stop auto buyers from purchasing SUVs. Still, anything less than real math could turn "0" if not into the new "green," all soft and meaningless, into something flabbier than it need be and less marketable than it should be.

Simple adjustments could be made in the calculations so the HERS scoring would be more meaningful. For example, a rater could go through all their calculations and when they're done add back a specific number of points for however much a house is bigger than the median. Points could be deducted for houses smaller than the median. Also, an electricity budget equal to a plug-in load that better reflects reality could be added to the reference home. As it is, the HERS standards give a single figure for annual kilowatt usage to only one appliance. The refrigerator in the reference home uses a hypothetical 775 kilowatt-hours annually and buying most Energy Star models will significantly improve on that number.

The same could be done with clothes washers, televisions, computers and a whole basket of plug-ins. It would likely make any estimate of energy use, like the KB Home EPG, more accurate, too. This way homeowners will have a better chance of not having to wait for 12 utility bills to pile up before they know the real score.

LEED

The Leadership in Energy and Environmental Design (LEED) system is about more than energy efficiency. It's a best practices for building that devotes more attention to rating how sustainable buildings are than measuring their energy efficiency. It cuts across the building landscape from residential to commercial much more so than HERS does and, in fact, relatively few single-family production homes have been rated.

Nevertheless, energy efficiency and renewable energy are where the most points by far are awarded. Depending on who's counting, it can be from a quarter to over a third of the total of 136 points. The HERS scoring is incorporated for calculating how many LEED points a home receives in that category. For example, a home with a HERS 0 rating gets 34 points. More energy efficiency points are awarded elsewhere in the system.

David Gottfried, the founder of the US Green Building Council (USGBC), a Washington, DC-based nonprofit organization, which developed and oversees the LEED ratings, claimed the highest rating ever, in 2009. He renovated a 94-year-old 1,440-square-foot Oakland, California, home that earned a score of 106.5, including the 34 for a HERS 0 — making his home, at least on paper, a net zero energy home.

But outside of setting records, striving to reach a single perfect score isn't the way LEED-rated homes are known. It's more like an Olympic or music industry rating system. A house that earns points that fall within a certain range is awarded, from least to best, a certified (45–59), silver (60–74), gold (75–89) or platinum (90–136) certification. LEED homes and the certification they received are listed on the USGBC's website.

Raters can be found on the website, too. The bigger the house and the higher the certification level sought, the more they will cost. One study of all types of LEED-rated buildings estimated the certification process cost between 1.5 and 3.1 percent of the buildings' production cost. Another study found that LEED certification cost $2.43 a square foot or over $5,000 for a median-sized home. Costs include fees paid to the USGBC and the rating providers.

Finally, a checklist of how to earn certification, followed by a detailed description of what everything on it means, is also available on the website. The checklist is broken up into eight categories. They are design (11 points), location (10), site selection (22), water efficiency (15), energy efficiency (38), material selection and waste management (16), indoor air quality (21) and education (3). The ratings also include the much-needed size adjustment. A small house gets as many as ten points taken off the score necessary to become certified (just 35) and beyond to silver, gold and platinum, while a large house may be required to have an additional ten or more to reach certification (55) and the other metal rankings.

Building small isn't the only way to win big points. There are a number of rich veins to mine on the way to reaching platinum. LEED has opportunities for double-dipping energy efficiency points. On top of the 34 points for a HERS 0, LEED awards four points for water-efficient showers and faucets (plus another two for toilets, not counted here), one of the easiest energy savings pick-ups whether it's for LEED, HERS or no rankings at all. Two points for not having a fireplace isn't just easy, it's a significant upfront cost saver. Passive design doesn't get much separate attention from LEED, but it's one more point to win.

The big ticket is air quality. Having a heat or energy recovery ventilator, standard in a zero energy home, may sweep up a good number of the 21 points allocated for air quality. A short well-insulated plumbing loop is another two points not necessarily part of HERS, but still a feature that contributes to energy efficiency.

The second biggest collection of points is the easiest to get, but the hardest to sell. The qualifying points are spread out and treated separately, but it comes down to the same thing. By reclaiming a structure or plot from the ever-expanding housing stock of needy vacant urban homes or lots (in Detroit, Buffalo, St. Louis, Pittsburgh, New Orleans, etc.) the developer may earn up to nineteen points. Most of the points awarded virtually define urban development. Two points can be earned by developing an infill, which is simply an empty space; such isolated tracts are about all that's available in cities. Another point is added if the plot has been previously developed, and while it's possible for a city infill to have no prior development, it's unlikely.

Other point winners are having access to water and sewer lines (1), various forms of public transportation and community resources (6) and being close to an open space (1). A small site (one-seventh of an acre), which is also about all that's available in cities at a reasonable price, gets another point and being surrounded by similar lots earns a healthy four additional points.

Two other tough sells are even easier to get, plus they'll save more than enough money to pay for the LEED rating. Doing without a garage will earn the homeowner three points and having permeable land around the house (no paved driveway or walkway from the street or sidewalk to the home's entrance) will add another four points.

A small zero energy home in a city has a lock on platinum.

The components of the LEED verification process make for a comprehensive list, but with the same glaring omission and the same prehistoric or at least pre-PC view of the world as RESNET. LEED leaves out televisions, computers and all that other plug-in electric stuff (though it does include clothes washers, which HERS doesn't). Another hidebound view is that while LEED goes to some length to award applicants points for using safe, renewable materials, it also awards points for adding toxic materials to the house, specifically the mercury found in compact fluorescent lights. LEED had nothing to say about LEDs at a time — 2011 — when non-toxic LED 60-watt incandescent-equivalent bulbs could be found almost anywhere.

However, the biggest shortcoming of both LEED and HERS is not taking costs into account. The single-minded focus on doing whatever it takes to pile up points may be the nature of the ratings game, but it's nevertheless a blow to making these energy efficient and sustainable homes more marketable because they favor buyers and builders with more financial resources.

The ratings game fills a void. It's a voluntary standard and status symbol used when strictly enforced super energy efficient building codes aren't in place. Not that the idea of developing a marketable home that actually produces as much energy as it uses is so different from a new home that earns a zero before the buyer even flips a light switch. Still, by paying as much attention to costs as to efficiency and consumption and setting a fixed, knowable goal we'll have the greatest potential for transitioning to where we need to be — living in what no longer has to be called a zero energy home, but just a home, sweet home.

Resources

Chapter 2

Finding the right tree height: Urban Tree Listing, State University of New York, Binghamton. Website: binghamton.edu/environmental-studies/urban-forestry/urban-tree-listing

Free trees source: Arbor Day Foundation.
Website: arborday.org/shopping

Free trees and plants source: Free Trees And Plants.Com.
Website: freetreesandplants.com

State foresters contacts: National Association of State Foresters.
Website: stateforesters.org

Forest Stewardship Council lumber directory: Forest Stewardship Council.
Website: info.fsc.org

Construction material recyclers directory: Construction Materials Recycling Association. Website: cdrecycling.org

Roof cost estimate calculator: New England Metal Roof.
Website: newenglandmetalroof.com

Low VOC paint directory. Greenguard. Website: greenguard.org

Low VOC paint directory. Green Seal. Website: greenseal.org

Chapter 3
Builders directory: Builders Challenge, Energy Efficiency and Renewable Energy, Department of Energy.
Website: eere.energy.gov/buildings
Builders directory: Energy Star, Department of Energy.
Website: energystar.gov
Projects directory: Research Projects, Building America, Department of Energy. Website: eere.energy.gov/buildings/building_america

Chapter 4
Insulation contractors directory: Insulation Contractors Association of America. Website: insulate.org
Spray foam contractors directory: Spray Polyurethane Foam Alliance.
Website: sprayfoam.org
Recycled rigid foam board insulation source: Insulation Depot.
Website: insulationdepot.com
Structural Insulated Panels membership contact: Structural Insulated Panel Association. Website: sips.org
Structural Insulated Panels directory by state: Panelized Home Builders.
Website: modularresource.com (click on "Green Building")
Insulating Concrete Form Association contractors: Insulating Concrete Form Association. Website: www.forms.org
Heat and energy recovery contractors and installers: North American Technician Excellence directory. Website: natex.org
Heat and energy recovery ventilator listings and specifications: Home Ventilating Institute. Website: hvi.org (click on "Consumers")

Chapter 5:
Energy savings and window type: Fact Sheet, Efficient Windows Collaborative. Website: efficientwindows.org
Triple pane windows volume discounts: High Performance Windows Volume Purchase program. Website: www.windowsvolumepurchase.org
Low-e window values: Efficient Windows Collaborative.
Website: efficientwindows.org
Windows directory: National Fenestration Rating Council.
Website: search.nfrc.org
Energy Star windows and door directories: Energy Star, Department of Energy. Website: energystar.gov

Chapter 6

US financial incentives directory: The Database of State Incentives for Renewable Energy. Website: dsireusa.org

Canadian financial incentives directory: Natural Resources Canada. Website: oee.nrcan.gc.ca

Net metering and interconnection rules and regulations: Interstate Renewable Energy Council. Website: newenergychoices.org

Chapter 7

Geothermal cost savings calculator: WaterFurnace. Website: waterfurnace.com

Geothermal heat pump installer directory: International Ground Source Heat Pump Association. Website: igshpa.okstate.edu

Energy Star geothermal heat pump listing: Energy Star, Department of Energy. Website: energystar.gov (Click on "Products")

Chapter 8

WaterSense fixtures directory: Environmental Protection Agency. Website: epa.gov/watersense (Click on "Products")

Energy Star clothes washer directory and calculator: Energy Star, Department of Energy. Website: energystar.gov (Click on "Products")

TopTen clothes washers rankings: TopTenUSA. Website: toptenusa.org

Energy Star dishwashers: Energy Star, Department of Energy. Website: energystar.gov (Click on "Products")

TopTen dishwashers rankings: TopTenUSA. Website: toptenusa.org

WaterSense-qualified toilets: WaterSense, Environmental Protection Agency. Website: epa.gov/watersense (Cllick on "Products")

Chapter 9

Refrigerator rankings: TopTenUSA. Website: toptenusa.org

Chapter 10

Sustainable flooring source: Green Floors. Website: greenfloors.com

Reclaimed wood sources. Website: Wood World: woodfibre.com

Build.Recycle.Net. Website: build.recycle.net

StickTrade.Com. Website: sticktrade.com

Chapter 11

Television rankings (small, large and medium): TopTenUSA. Website: toptenusa.org

Energy Star computer listing: Energy Star, Department of Energy.
  Website: energystar.gov (Click on "Products")
Computer rankings (desktops, laptops and monitors): TopTenUSA.
  Website: toptenusa.org

Chapter 12
Certified photovoltaic installers directory: North American Board Certified
  Energy Practitioners. Website: nabcep.org
Sunlight calculator: PVwatt, version 1, National Renewable Energy
  Laboratory. Website: nrel.gov/rredc (Click on "PVWatts")
Certified solar modules list: Certified Modules, Certification and
  Testing, Florida Solar Energy Center. Website: fsec.ucf.edu (Click on
  "Certification & Testing")
Inverter list: Go Solar, California Energy Commission.
  Website: gosolarcalifornia.org
Photovoltaic costs and payback calculator: Sharp Clean Power Estimator.
  Website: sharpusa.cleanpowerestimator.com
Photovoltaic costs and payback calculator: Clean Power Estimator,
  Connecticut Clean Energy Fund. Website: clean-power.com/ccef
Photovoltaic costs and payback calculator: In My Backyard, National
  Renewable Energy Laboratory. Website: nrel.gov/eis/imby
Photovoltaic costs and payback calculator: Go Solar, California Energy
  Commission. Website: cec.cleanpowerestimator.com

Chapter 13
HERS raters and auditors directory: Finding Raters and Auditors,
  RESNET. Website: resnet.us
HERS standards: Mortgage Industry National Home Energy Rating
  Standards. Website: resnet.us/standards
LEED standards, raters directory and certified homes by state and by
  rating: US Green Building Council. Website: usgbc.org

Notes and References

Chapter 1

Savings of about $2,200 annually in 2009 (Typical House memo, Lawrence Berkeley National Laboratory, 2009): energystar.gov/index. cfm?c=products.pr_pie

A home's value is said to increase an average of $20 for each $1 decrease in the annual utility bill (according to the *Appraisal Journal,* October 1998): resnet.us/ratings/overview/resources/appraisal/default.htm

Four homes have achieved net zero energy over twelve months (GreenBuildingAdvisor.com, March 10, 2011): greenbuildingadvisor. com/blogs/dept/green-building-news/vermont-house-wins-10000-net-zero-energy-prize

130 million residences in the US in 2009 (US Census, American Housing Survey, Introductory Characteristics, 2009): census.gov/hhes/www/ housing/ahs/ahs09/ahs09.html

In most years, more than a million new single-family homes are added to the housing stock (US Census, New Residential Construction, 2009): census.gov/const/www/newresconstindex.html

Major builders like Pulte, Centex and Shea took stabs at building prototype zero energy homes ("Large-Production Home Builder Experience with Zero Energy Homes," Barbara C. Farhar, Timothy C. Coburn and Megan Murphy, Case Studies, Toolbase, National Association of Home Builders, National Renewable Energy Laboratory, Center for Energy Research, July 2004) toolbase.org/PDF/CaseStudies/ZEH_NRELfarhar1.pdf; ("Moving Towards Zero Energy Homes," National Renewable Energy Laboratory, US Department of Energy, December 2003) nrel.gov/docs/fy04osti/35317.pdf; and ("UNLV Zero or Near-Zero Energy House Projects in Las Vegas," Robert Boehm, Center for Energy Research, UNLV, February 3, 2009) dodfuelcell.cecer.army.mil/rd/NZE_Workshop/ 1a_Boehm.pdf

Only one million were built (Major Milestones, Energy Star, Environmental Protection Agency, US Department of Energy, 2010): energystar.gov/index.cfm?c=about.ab_milestones

First-Time Home Buyer study ("Characteristics of First-Time Home Buyers," Elliot Eisenberg, National Association of Home Builders, January 23, 2008): nahb.org/generic.aspx?sectionID=734&genericContentID=88533&channelID=311

Green Day gets stoned (*Simpsons Movie*, 2007): video-clips/tkcf98/simpsons-the-movie-exclusive-dvd-clip

Median square feet, US single-family house (US Census, 2010): census.gov/const/C25Ann/sftotalmedavgsqft.pdf

Chapter 2

Largest Home Builders, 2009 (Builder Magazine, 2010): builderonline.com/builder100/2009.aspx

Land density, 2000 (US Census, 2000): census.gov/population/www/censusdata/density.html

Energy savings attributable to having a southern exposure ("Turn to Solar for Lower Heating Costs," Oikos, Energy Source Builder, December 1995): oikos.com/esb/42/solar.html

Architect unemployment (Architectural Record, October 25, 2010): archrecord.construction.com/news/daily/archives/2010/10/101025real_employment.asp

Planting trees for energy efficiency ("Landscaping for Energy Efficiency," National Renewable Energy Laboratory, April 1995): nrel.gov/docs/legosti/old/16632.pdf

Five percent of US forests FSC-certified ("Assessing USGBC's Policy Options for Forest Certification and the Use of Wood and Other Bio-based Materials," a summary report prepared by the Yale Program on Forest Policy and Governance, Yale University, February 25, 2008): yale.edu/forestcertification/YPFPGUSGBCFinal3.pdf

Market share of various sidings (US Census, 2010): census.gov/const/C25Ann/sftotalexwallmat.pdf

Ten of eleven tons of asphalt goes to landfills (Northeast Recycling Council, 2007): nerc.org/documents/asphalt.pdf

Market share of garages in new homes (US Census, 2010): census.gov/const/C25Ann/sftotalparking.pdf

Chapter 3

Solar capacity, by state (US Solar Market Trends, Interstate Renewable Energy Council, July 27, 2010): irecusa.org/wp-content/uploads/2010/07/IREC-Solar-Market-Trends-Report-2010_7-27-10_web1.pdf

Chapter 4

Spray foam video (YouTube, 2011): youtube.com/watch?v=VFjxWdPPY1Q

Structural insulated panels' estimated market share of housing market is between one percent and two percent (News Release, The Structural Insulated Panel Association, July 1, 2010): sips.org/content/news/index.cfm?PageId=310

Concrete uses five times as much energy to produce than used in harvesting lumber (Treehugger, January 6, 2011): treehugger.com/files/2006/11/concrete_can_it_1.php

Insulating concrete forms' estimated market share of housing market is around four percent (Newsletter, Portland Cement Association, November/December 2007): cement.org/homes/ch_newsletter2007-11&12.asp#Market

Fiberglass loses 28 percent of its R-value ("Fiberglass batts — labeled vs. Installed Performance," Oak Ridge National Laboratory, 1998): dccnisswa.com/uploads/Fiberglass_insul_loses_R-value.pdf

Chapter 5

Comparison shopping for doors (*Consumer Reports*, November 2007): consumerreports.org/cro/home-garden/home-improvement/hardware-building-supplies/doors-entry/entry-doors-1004/overview/

Chapter 6

States with most solar capacity have offered best financial incentives (US Solar Market Trends, Interstate Renewable Energy Council, July 2010): ases.org/papers/057.pdf

2010 State Energy Efficiency Scorecard Ranking (American Council for an Energy Efficient Economy, 2011): aceee.org/energy-efficiency-sector/state-policy/aceee-state-scorecard-ranking

Chapter 7

Central air conditioning and room air conditioning, historic comparison (American House Survey, US Department of Housing and Urban Development, 2009): huduser.org/portal/datasets/ahs/ahsdata09.html

Toby Keith and other celebrity users of geothermal heat pumps ("Heat from the Earth to Warm Your Hearth," by Barry Rehfeld, *The New York Times*, January 1, 2006): nytimes.com/2006/01/01/business/yourmoney/01 thermal. html?_r=1&scp=1&sq=barry%20rehfeld%20geothermal&st=cse

Geothermal heat pump shipments (Energy Information Administration, December 2010): eia.gov/cneaf/solar.renewables/page/heatpumps/heatpumps.html

Natural Gas Prices (Energy Information Administration, May 31, 2011): eia.doe.gov/dnav/ng/ng_pri_sum_dcu_nus_m.htm

Ground source heat pump shipments, by state (Energy Information Administration, December 2010): eia.doe.gov/cneaf/solar.renewables/page/rea_data/table4_6.pdf

Chapter 8

Shower uses 20 gallons ("Shower vs. Bath," Consumer Energy Center, California Energy Commission, 2011): consumerenergycenter.org/myths/shower_vs_bath.html

Using four gallons of water to wash hands and face (Water Heaters, Cooperative Extension Service, University of Illinois, June 1994): web.aces.uiuc.edu/vista/pdf_pubs/WATRHTRS.PDF

Clothes washer uses 30 gallons per cycle (Energy Star, Department of Energy, 2011): energystar.gov/index.cfm?fuseaction=clotheswash.display_column_definitions

Dishwasher uses ten gallons per cycle (Energy Star, Department of Energy, 2011): energystar.gov/index.cfm?fuseaction=find_a_product.showProductGroup&pgw_code=DW

Clothes washer used 400 times annually (Energy Star, Department of Energy, 2011): energystar.gov/index.cfm?fuseaction=find_a_product. showProductGroup&pgw_code=CW

Dishwasher used 215 times annually (Cool the Earth, 2010): cooltheearth.org/action_coupons/show/54/

Clothes washers in homes, 84 percent; dishwashers in homes, 66 percent (Selected Equipment, American Housing Survey, US Census, 2009): energystar.gov/index.cfm?fuseaction=find_a_product.showProduct Group&pgw_code=DW

Clothes washer and dishwasher household rank in hot water use ("The End Uses of Hot Water in Single Family Homes from Flow Trace Analysis," William B. DeOreo, P.E., Peter W. Mayer, Aquacraft, Inc., Water Engineering and Management, 2001): aquacraft.com/sites/default/files/ pub/DeOreo-(2001)-Disaggregated-Hot-Water-Use-in-Single-Family-Homes-Using-Flow-Trace-Analysis.pdf

Number of bathrooms (Characteristics of New Housing, US Census, 2010): census.gov/const/C25Ann/sftotalbaths.pdf

Drought and shortage prospects ("Steps to Take Before the Collective Well Runs Dry," Barry Rehfeld, *The New York Times,* November 13, 2005): query.nytimes.com/gst/fullpage.html?res=9801E4DF133EF930A25752 C1A9639C8B63&scp=2&sq=barry%20rehfeld%20and%20water&st=cse

"Black market" shower heads episode (*Seinfeld,* 1996): youtube.com/watch?v=dlrtQb24Qxw

Use cold water for clothes washing (Laundry, American Council for An Energy Efficient Economy, June 2010): aceee.org/consumer/laundry

Chapter 9

Percent of homes with refrigerators, stove/oven, clothes dryer and microwave and percent with electric stove/oven and clothes dryers (US Census, 2005): eia.doe.gov/emeu/recs/recs2005/hc2005_tables/ hc9homeappliance/pdf/tablehc10.9.pdf

Refrigerator size from 1980 to 2007 and Energy Star refrigerator market share 1997 to 2008 (Refrigerator Market Profile, Department of Energy, December 2009): energystar.gov/ia/partners/manuf_res/downloads/ Refrigerator_Market_Profile_2009.pdf

Market share of refrigerators, by configuration (Analysis of Amended Energy Conservation Standards for Residential Refrigerator-Freezers,

Department of Energy, October 2005): eere.energy.gov/buildings/
appliance_standards/pdfs/refrigerator_report_1.pdf

LED bulbs costing a few dollars ("In Battle of the Bulbs, One Based on TV
Tubes," Eric Taub, *The New York Times*, March 21, 2011): nytimes.com/
2011/03/21/technology/21lamp.html?_r=1&scp=2&sq=compact%20
fluorescent&st=cse

Chapter 10

Floor covering prices (Components: Flooring, The Minnesota Green
Affordable Housing Guide, 2007): greenhousing.umn.edu/comp_
flooring.html

Carpeting made of recycled material, R-value (Carpet and Cushion,
Radiant Panel Association, 2011): radiantpanelassociation.org/i4a/pages/
index.cfm?pageid=143

Copper in 41 percent of homes; PEX 19 percent (Research Works, HUD
User, Department of Housing and Urban Development, November
2007): huduser.org/periodicals/Researchworks/nov_07/RW_
vol4num10t2.html

The plastics scene from *The Graduate* (YouTube, 2011): youtube.com/
watch?v=PSxihhBzCjk

Chapter 11

George Carlin's *Stuff* routine (YouTube, 2011): youtube.com/watch?v=
MvgN5gCuLac

Televisions, computers, printers in homes, 2005 (Home Electronics
Characteristics, Energy Information Administration, 2005):
eia.doe.gov/emeu/recs/recs2005/hc2005_tables/hc11homeelectronics/
pdf/tablehc6.11.pdf

Televisions, computers and printers in homes, 2001 (Housing
Characteristics, Type of Housing, Appliances, Energy Information
Administration, 2001): eia.gov/emeu/recs/recs2001/hc_pdf/appl/hc5-
5a_ownerunits2001.pdf

Consumer electronics consume 11 percent of residential electricity in 2006
(Energy Consumption by Consumer Electronics in US Residences,
Consumer Electronics Association, January 2007): ce.org/pdf/Energy
%20Consumption%20by%20CE%20in%20U.S.%20Residences%20
(January%202007).pdf

Energy used by computers and consumer electronics will triple by 2030

("Gadgets and Gigawatts," International Energy Agency, May 2009):
iea.org/W/bookshop/FlyerGadgetsGigawatts.pdf

Plug-ins used between 15 to 30 percent of the residential electricity used
in Wisconsin ("Electricity Savings Opportunities for Home Electronics
and Other Plug-In Devices in Minnesota Homes," Energy Center of
Wisconsin, 2010): ecw.org/resource_detail.php?resultid=430

Chapter 12

Number of residential grid-connected photovoltaic installations and their
size (US Solar Market Trends, Interstate Renewable Energy Council,
July 2010): irecusa.org/wp-content/uploads/2010/07/IREC-Solar-
Market-Trends-Report-2010_7-27-10_web1.pdf

Solar panel ladder lift (YouTube, 2011): youtube.com/watch?v=
xZDhY3Rj6h4

Electric utility rates, by state (Average Retail Price, Energy Information
Administration, December 2010): eia.doe.gov/cneaf/electricity/epm/
table5_6_a.html

Solar module prices per watt (Module Pricing, Facts and Figures,
Solarbuzz, 2011): solarbuzz.com/facts-and-figures/retail-price-
environment/module-prices

Net metering grades ("Freeing the Grid," Interstate Renewable Energy
Council, 2010): newenergychoices.org/uploads/FreeingTheGrid2010.pdf

Distributed versus central photovoltaic generation ("Relative Merits of
Distributed vs. Central Photovoltaic Generation," California Energy
Commission, April 7, 2004): energy.ca.gov/reports/2004-09-27_500-
04-065.PDF

Reasons for developing distributed generation ("The Potential Benefits of
Distributed Generation and the Rate-Related Issues that May Impede
its Expansion," Department of Energy, February 2007): oe.energy.gov/
DocumentsandMedia/1817_Report_final.pdf

Electricity transmission loss data (State Electricity Profiles 2008, Energy
Information Administration, March 2010): eia.doe.gov/cneaf/electricity/
st_profiles/sep2008.pdf

Homes suitable for wind power (AWEA Small Wind Turbine Global
Market Study, American Wind Energy Association, 2010): awea.org/
learnabout/smallwind/upload/2010_AWEA_Small_Wind_Turbine_
Global_Market_Study.pdf

Chapter 13

What LEED and Energy Star add to commercial property values ("Green
Noise or Green Value?," Franz Fuerst and Patrick M. McAllister, Social
Science Research Network, July 15, 2008): papers.ssrn.com/sol3/papers.
cfm?abstract_id=1140409

HERS inaccuracy ("Accuracy of Home Energy Rating Systems," Jeff Ross
Stein, Lawrence Berkeley National Laboratory, June 1997): eetd.lbl.gov/
EA/Reports/40394/40394.pdf

Large home advantage in HERS scoring ("Analysis of Energy
Consumption, Rating Score, and House Size," Duncan Prahl, Ibacos, US
Green Building Council, October 20, 2003): usgbc.org/Docs/Archive/
MediaArchive/310_Prahl_PA772.pdf

Cost of HERS Rating ("Review of Home Energy Ratings and Labeling of
Energy Performance of Homes," Steve Baden, RESNET, Oregon Energy
Performance Scores Taskforce Meeting, March 11, 2010): oregon.gov/
energy/cons/eps/docs/SteveBadenOregonLabellingPresentation.pdf?ga=t

RESNET Survey on Costs, 2009 ("National Average Cost of Home
Energy Ratings", RESNET, February 27, 2009): resnet.us/hotnews/
Report_on_Cost_of_Ratings.pdf

Energy Efficiency difference between 2006 and 2009, International Energy
Conservation Code ECC ("Reducing the Energy Use of Houses,"
William Post, Coalition for Energy Solutions, December 2010):
coalitionforenergysolutions.org/reducing_energy_use_wp_1.pdf

Difference between HERS projected and actual energy use ("Accuracy of
Home Energy Rating Systems," Jeff Stein and Alan Meier, Lawrence
Berkeley National Laboratory, January 11, 1999): eetd.lbl.gov/ea/
akmeier/pdf/ross-stein-meier-audits-accuracy-99.pdf

LEED fees, 2003 ("Analyzing the Cost of Obtaining LEED Certification,"
Northbridge Environmental Management Consultants, The American
Chemistry Council, April 16, 2003): cleanair-coolplanet.org/for_
communities/LEED_links/AnalyzingtheCostofLEED.pdf

LEED fees, 2011 ("LEED for Homes Rating System," Sustainable Cities
Institute, Home Depot Foundation, 2011): sustainablecitiesinstitute.org/
view/page.basic/class/feature.class/Lesson_LEED_Homes_Rating_
System

Index

A

ABS (Acrylonitrile Butadiene Styrene), 138

ACCA (Air Conditioning Contractors of America), 99

ACEEE (American Council for an Energy-Efficient Economy), 87, 116

Acer, 148

air conditioners, 97–99, 120

air-conditioning costs, 46

air source heat pumps (ASHPs), 45, 101, 102–103

air source hot water heat pumps, 121

AL (air leakage), 77

Alabama, trees, 29

Alston 658, 113

aluminum window frames, 81

American Council for an Energy-Efficient Economy (ACEEE), 87, 116

American Foursquare design, 22

American Institute of Architects, 23

American Society of Heating, Refrigerating and Air-Conditioning Engineers, 6

American Standard, 70, 113, 122

American Water Works Association, 110

Amur Maple, 29

Anasazi cliff dwellers, 73

apartments, size of, 23–24

appliances, 169

  See also specific appliance

The Appraisal Journal, 4

Arbor Day Foundation, 29

Arcata, California, 165

architects, 22

argon windows, 79

Ariston, 120

Arizona, leasing panels, 94

Arkansas, incentives, 89

Artistic Homes, 40, 47–49

Ashland, Oregon, 90

ASHPs (air source heat pumps), 45, 101, 102–103

Asia, wood from, 31

Asko, 116

asphalt, for driveways, 37–38

asphalt shingles, 33–34

attics, insulation, 58, 59, 63, 64, 67

Austria, 19–20

awning windows, 80

About the Author

BARRY REHFELD IS A WRITER, editor and teacher. His writing career began in the eighties while working as reporter-researcher for *Time* magazine. He wrote freelance articles for *Esquire, Rolling Stone* and *The New York Times* and co-authored a book on Wall Street, *The New Crowd.* He subsequently became a senior writer at *Institutional Investor* and the features editor at *American Banker. Home Sweet Zero Energy Home* grew out of a number of freelance articles he wrote for the *Times* from 2005 to 2007 on energy efficiency and renewable energy and his web site, begun in 2008, *Zeroenergyintelligence. com.* He is also a physics teacher and lives with his wife in an apartment in New York where they use approximately 4,000 kilowatts annually.

If you have enjoyed *Home Sweet Zero Energy Home*,
you might also enjoy other

BOOKS TO BUILD A NEW SOCIETY

Our books provide positive solutions for people who want to
make a difference. We specialize in:

**Sustainable Living • Green Building • Peak Oil
Renewable Energy • Environment & Economy
Natural Building & Appropriate Technology
Progressive Leadership • Resistance and Community
Educational & Parenting Resources**

For a full list of NSP's titles, please call 1-800-567-6772 *or check out our website* at:
www.newsociety.com

NEW SOCIETY PUBLISHERS
Deep Green for over 30 years